SCOTLAND FOREVER!

The Scots Greys at Waterloo

Iain Gale

BIRLINN

First published in 2015 by Birlinn Ltd
West Newington House
10 Newington Road
Edinburgh
EH9 1QS
www.birlinn.co.uk

ISBN: 978 1 84341 068 3

British Library Cataloguing in Publication Data
A catalogue record for this book is available from the
British Library

Typeset in Sabon at Birlinn

Printed and bound in Great Britain by Bell & Bain Ltd

Contents

Foreword

by

Brigadier Simon Allen
Colonel, The Royal Scots Dragoon Guards

The Royal Scots Dragoon Guards is Scotland's senior regiment and her only regular cavalry. The Regiment retains the captured eagle of the 45th Regiment as the centrepiece of its cap badge and celebrates the Battle of Waterloo annually as one of two principal battle honours. The story of the battle has been recounted in numerous publications and examined from every angle. But the military history of this period is not always presented in such a way as to appeal to everyone, and it can appear dry to those unfamiliar with the significance of the events of nineteenth-century Europe.

In his lively and very readable book, military historian and novelist Iain Gale has enthusiastically and energetically embraced his subject to give us a very colourful description of the part played by the Scots Greys in the Battle of Waterloo, as it has come to be known. He brings to life the characters of this unfolding drama, with all their imperfections and foibles, in a way that makes them readily identifiable to readers in the twenty-first century. The privations and lifestyle of the Scottish soldier nevertheless remain a million miles away from the profligate excesses of the present day, reminding the reader of his good fortune in not having been born in those times.

Whether or not the charge of the Union Brigade turned out exactly as Wellington had hoped it would, there is little doubt that the actions of the Scots Greys contributed to victory over Napoleon and the end of his dreams of political liberalisation in Europe. Britain grew stronger and richer as a result, and the charge of the Greys became one of the many romantic tales to emanate from the battle and was recorded by various artists, most notably by Lady Butler in her painting 'Scotland Forever!'.

Today the Regiment is based in its native Scotland in an essentially expeditionary role that would be familiar to its antecedents. The nature of warfare is constantly changing and yet, whatever the future may bring, I have little doubt that the Royal Scots Dragoon Guards will rise to the challenges, as did their forbears, bolstered by the justifiable belief that the Regiment remains *Second to None.*

Author's Note

This book has been in my head for some forty years. Ever since when, as a boy, I was taken to see Dino de Laurentis's spectacular film *Waterloo* in 1970, I have been fascinated (some would say obsessed) by the battle and campaign. I have written about it, studied the men who fought in it, refought it myself in miniature, visited the battlefield countless times and guided tours around it ranging from parties of schoolchildren to 32 serving US army officers on a TEWT. After all those years the key episodes still stand out. The defence of Hougoumont and La Haye Sainte, the great French cavalry charges against the chequerboard Allied squares, the assault of the Old Guard and, not least, the attack of d'Erlon's Corps and its destruction by the redcoats of Picton's Division and the British heavy cavalry.

The charge of the Scots Greys at Waterloo is probably the most iconic of all images of the battle. Thanks to Lady Butler's hugely inspiring, if inaccurate, painting of 1881, *Scotland for Ever!*, it resonates in the public imagination every time the battle is mentioned.

It was early on in the course of my reading that I began to realise that Lady Butler's image was far from true to life. The Greys, it seems from contemporary accounts, did not charge. The fastest they got was a gallop. Yet, far from shattering my boyhood dreams of glory this only made me want to enquire further. How did they defeat the French? How could the Union Brigade of just 1,200 cavalry destroy an entire 15,000-man army corps? Was it true that they went too far and were in their own turn destroyed? Above all, who were they, these extraordinary Scottish horsemen?

Thanks to the recent research of Stuart Mellor in his invaluable book *Greys' Ghosts*, we are closer to knowing just that. But I wanted to go a stage further: to put the men in the context not only of the 'charge' but of the whole campaign and the later stages of the battle. What was the truth about the taking of the French eagle which forms the centrepiece of the regimental museum in Edinburgh Castle. And who was the man who had taken it, the hero, Ensign Ewart, who lies entombed on the Castle Esplanade?

Using memoirs, diaries and letters written by some of the men who were there, I was able to piece together the events of the four days of the campaign with more accuracy I believe than ever before. I would like to think that I may also have laid to rest some old rumours and arguments.

That said, however, no history of a battle is ever wholly correct and the reader must remain aware that even such apparently truthful primary sources as those used by me in this work still have their biases, prejudices and personal agendas.

I have had to be careful too not to over-embroider. As a writer of military fiction there is a tendency for me to invent dialogue and to put into the heads of the protagonists thoughts which I might suppose to be there.

I have endeavoured not to do either of these things. Ninety percent of the dialogue in this book is as it was reported in the original sources. All the rest is careful guesswork based upon my knowledge of the period.

Doubtless some readers will find fault in some details and for this I apologise. I am always happy to stand corrected and welcome all correspondence.

Lastly a word on the title. 'Scotland forever' was, according to several sources, the cry given up as the Greys went to meet the French, and it was naturally taken up by the men of the 92nd Gordon Highlanders as the great grey horses pushed through their ranks to get at the enemy. The Caton-Woodville image of the leaping Highlander holding on to the dragoon's stirrup must be taken with a pinch of salt. But it seems certain that in their haste to be on the French, some of the 92nd did try to hold the legs of the cavalrymen. Either way it is a fitting title for a book which commemorates perhaps the greatest feat to date of Scotland's only cavalry regiment.

Acknowledgements

Over the past two years I have come to know the regimental descendents of the Greys who fought at Waterloo, being privileged to have been asked to sit on the Waterloo 200 Committee of the regiment's present day incarnation, the Royal Scots Dragoon Guards. I can honestly say that I have never before been a member of quite so convivial a committee, and through my acquaintance with the officers and men of today's Scottish cavalry, both retired and those who at the time were still serving on the front line in Afghanistan, I have come to understand something of the spirit and strength of character which surely held together the regiment at Waterloo in its finest and ultimately most perilous hour.

I would like to thank in particular Major Robin Maclean, curator and librarian of the regimental museum at Edinburgh Castle for his tireless help in finding source material and his suggestions throughout the process. I should also like to thank Brigadier Mel Jamieson for his enthusiastic support in the project and of course Brigadier Simon Allen, Colonel of the Regiment, for his foreword to this book.

Other members of the Committee who also deserve my thanks include Captain Rory Maclachlan, Major Jamie Erskine, Lt Colonel Mike Bullen and regimental historian Stephen Wood for his advice on casualties during the battle. On this last point, while the figures on which I have settled for losses at Waterloo are 105 dead and 93 wounded, these by no means represent only the men lost by the Greys as a consequence of the attack on d'Erlon's corps. The regiment had suffered several casualties on 17 June, and on the18th on its return from the valley, stood for another six hours of fighting and engaged in several further charges. All this time it continued to take casualties, and I hope that I have made this attrition plain in the course of the text.

Lastly I would like to thank my publisher Hugh Andrew who believed in the book from day one, and my editor Tom Johnstone, for their guidance and advice.

Iain Gale, Edinburgh 2015

Dedication

To the officers and men of the
2nd Royal North British Dragoons
who fell in the Waterloo campaign
16–18 June 1815

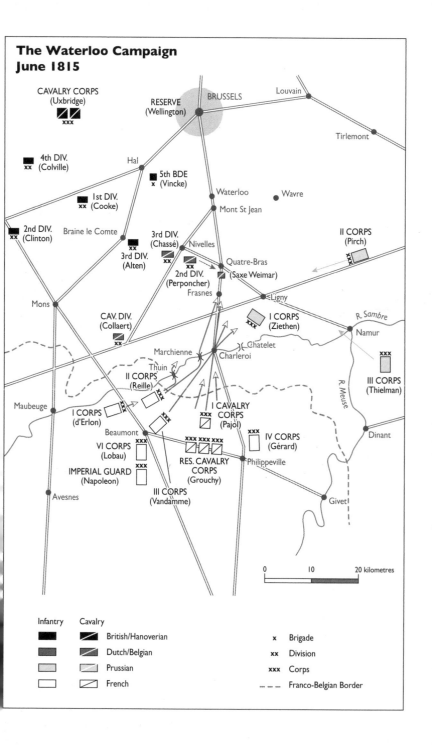

The Waterloo Campaign
June 1815

CAVALRY CORPS
(Uxbridge)

BRUSSELS

RESERVE
(Wellington)

Louvain

Tirlemont

4th DIV.
(Colville)

Hal

5th BDE
(Vincke)

Waterloo

Wavre

1st DIV.
(Cooke)

Mont St Jean

II CORPS
(Pirch)

2nd DIV.
(Clinton)

Braine le Comte

3rd DIV.
(Chassé)

Nivelles

3rd DIV.
(Alten)

2nd DIV.
(Perponcher)

Quatre-Bras
(Saxe Weimar)

Mons

Frasnes

Ligny

R. Sambre

CAV. DIV.
(Collaert)

I CORPS
(Ziethen)

Namur

Marchienne

Chatelet

III CORPS
(Thielman)

Thuin

Charleroi

II CORPS
(Reille)

R. Meuse

Maubeuge

I CORPS
(d'Erlon)

I CAVALRY
CORPS
(Pajol)

Dinant

Beaumont

VI CORPS
(Lobau)

RES. CAVALRY
CORPS
(Grouchy)

IV CORPS
(Gérard)

Philippeville

IMPERIAL GUARD
(Napoleon)

Avesnes

III CORPS
(Vandamme)

Givet

0   10   20 kilometres

Infantry   Cavalry

British/Hanoverian   x   Brigade

Dutch/Belgian   xx   Division

Prussian   xxx   Corps

French   - - - Franco-Belgian Border

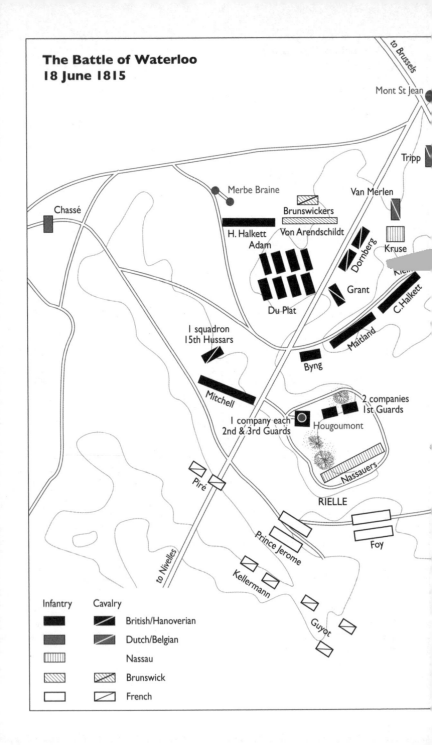

The Battle of Waterloo
18 June 1815

to Brussels

Mont St Jean

Tripp

Merbe Braine

Van Merlen

Brunswickers

Chassé

Von Arendschildt

H. Halkett

Dornberg

Kruse

Adam

Kiel...

Grant

C.Halkett

Du Plat

Maitland

I squadron
15th Hussars

Byng

Mitchell

2 companies
1st Guards

I company each
2nd & 3rd Guards

Hougoumont

Nassauers

Piré

RIELLE

Prince Jerome

Foy

to Nivelles

Kellermann

Guyot

Infantry	Cavalry	
■	◣	British/Hanoverian
■	◣	Dutch/Belgian
▥		Nassau
▨	▨	Brunswick
☐	◿	French

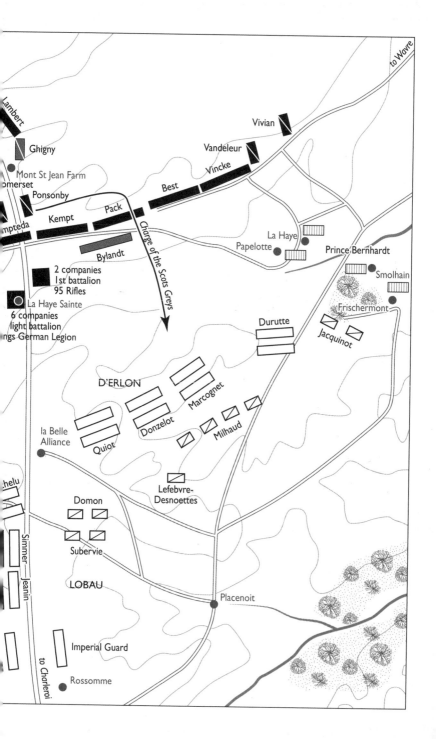

1

Opening Moves

Napoleon Bonaparte escaped from exile on the island of Elba on the 26th of February, 1815. He had with him only 1,000 men. Landing on the south coast of France at Golfe-Juan near Antibes, the man who as the Emperor of France had once ruled most of Europe led his tiny army north.

At Besançon on the 10th of March he was confronted by Marshal Michel Ney, one of his most trusted generals, and a regiment of foot. Ney had promised the French King, the Bourbon Louis XVIII, to return with Napoleon 'in an iron cage'. But such was his former master's magnetism that Ney's troops went over to Napoleon, and Ney himself joined them.

Following a triumphant march through France, the Emperor arrived in Paris on the 20th of March at the head of two Divisions comprising some ten thousand men.

News of his escape was laughed at by the allied generals and politicians attending the peace negotiations in Vienna; until they realised that it was not in fact a joke. Then panic gripped Europe, as people wondered if this man would plunge them into another twenty years of world war.

In fact Napoleon wanted peace, and tried his best to obtain it. He wrote letters to the Prince Regent of Britain and the Russian Emperor, proposing a peaceful resolution of the conflict. But the Allies steadfastly refused his entreaties and declared war not on the French nation, but on Napoleon himself.

His response was swift and effective. Within two months Napoleon had assembled an army of half a million men, with some 200,000 in the field along with 360 cannon. They were mostly veterans and loyal to the man who for two decades had led them to glory.

It was a remarkable feat and it almost bankrupted France. It cost 5 million francs a month to supply the Armée du Nord, and they also needed new weapons and horses. Across France the munitions factories turned out 40,000 muskets a month, although bayonets were more of a problem.

Uniforms too were a mess. Regiments broke the Royalist *fleurs de lys* off their shakos, and some managed to find brass eagles with which to replace them. In particular there was not enough body armour to supply Napoleon's legendary cuirassiers, his elite heavy cavalry, and one regiment went into battle without it.

Horses too were in short supply. The Emperor's disastrous campaign in Russia had cost no less than 180,000 horses and there just weren't enough of them. Nevertheless, by June 1815 Napoleon was able to field an impressive army which to any observer would have had at least the appearance of the Grand Armée of 1805.

*

His opponents had three times as many men on which to call. 200,000 Russians under Barclay de Tolley were marching to the French border along with the same number of Austrians under Schwarzenberg.

The Duke of Wellington, victor of the Peninsula, had managed to scrape together 112,000 men at his headquarters in the Netherlands and 130,000 Prussians under the veteran Marshal Blücher had marched to join him from Germany. But importantly the armies were split, and Napoleon knew this. He had 123,000 men in the north of France with another 100,000 across the nation.

The only way to tackle his enemies was piecemeal, dividing Wellington and Blücher and dealing with each army in turn. To Napoleon's advantage he was fighting in his own territory on interior lines and thus needed fewer men. He also had other considerable advantages.

Wellington's army was not what he would have wished for. After six years of campaigning in Spain and Portugal, it was run down. Britain had also just fought and lost a war in America during which, famously, British troops had burned down the White House.

Most of the Peninsular veterans had been sent home, to fight in America or to suppress rioting in Ireland. The last thing that Britain wanted was a European war.

Wellington's British army, a total of just 15,000 men, comprised 25 battalions of infantry and six regiments of horse, but many were at half strength. In addition to this, many of them were untried in battle and some were very young.

Apart from these troops he had an army of allies: Hanoverians, Nassauers, Brunswickers, Dutch and Belgians, making up the grand total of 112,000. A month before the battle of Waterloo, he called it 'an infamous army, very weak and ill equipped and a very inexperienced staff.'

Of course, using his experience, Wellington did everything he could to strengthen this force. He brigaded green regiments with veterans. In each army corps he placed

Dutch-Belgian divisions alongside British. The reserve was made up of British, Dutch and Germans.

The historian J. W. Fortescue describes how this filtered down to the brigades:

> In every British Division except the First, foreigners were blended with redcoats. Altens and Clinton's had each one brigade of British, one of the German Legion and one of Hanoverians. Picton's and Colville's had each two brigades of British and one of Hanoverians . . . In Cooke's division of British footguards, the three young battalions were stiffened by one old one from the Peninsula.

Blücher's army was similarly unimpressive. Prussia too was impoverished by war, but the King of Prussia ordered mobilisation and managed to get 130,000 men in the field. The staff was split between Blücher leading from the front and von Gniesenau, the mastermind who formed the strategy.

*

Napoleon took the initiative and on 15 June split his own army. The left wing of 50,000 men and 100 guns was to be commanded by Ney; the right, of the same strength, by Marshal Grouchy. Napoleon himself would have the reserve with the Imperial Guard infantry, an infantry corps and a reserve cavalry corps, 30,000 men with 150 guns. He would be able to detach units from each of these three wings as required.

His staff were vital. Soult was his chief of staff, with

Ney and Grouchy as the senior commanders supported by the Minister of War, Davout. But some key men from his early campaigns were missing. There was no Lasnes, no Massena and no Murat. Worse than this, the staff were plagued by mistrust and jealousy.

And another key figure was missing. His chief of staff Berthier, who had been with him through his campaigns, had died in strange circumstances after falling from a window in Bamberg, Bavaria, on 1 June. So Napoleon had to make do with Soult, who had been beaten by Wellington in Spain. He was best known as a plunderer of fine art, and after Napoleon's first abdication in 1814 had been Louis XVIII's Minister of War. Soult was not what Berthier had been, an efficient military secretary. He was a battlefield general and was miscast by Napoleon.

From the start, though, whatever the Emperor's deficiencies, the Allies were on the back foot. They knew that they needed to attack, but they would have to wait for the Russians and Austrians for this to be possible. Wellington prayed that Napoleon would not attack before this. The only thing they could do was post pickets to try to ensure they knew where the French were.

Wellington was increasingly paranoid that Napoleon might try a feint and believed that his adversary would try to cut his lines of communication to the sea at Ostend. But Blücher's lines of communication were on the east, into Germany, and the old Feld-Marschal had to protect these. So even though they had already agreed that if one were attacked the other would help, the Allied commanders had their own conflicting demands.

*

The moment of truth came on 15 June, when at 3.30 am the Prussians were attacked at Thuin, south of Charleroi across the Belgian border.

The French had been on the move since 3 am, with light cavalry scouts in front and an endless train of marching men and wagons. Soon there was a bottleneck, and other things began to go wrong. General Vandamme did not receive his movement orders as the messenger fell off his horse and broke a leg. A general deserted to the allies. But battle had been joined. Jerome Bonaparte's 6th Division of the 2nd Corps opened fire on a unit of Prussian Landwehr in Ziethen's I Corps, and as the pressure was applied, the Prussians began to pull back.

By morning the French were in Charleroi fighting what remained of the Prussian resistance and Napoleon sat down beside a local inn and watched the columns march past on their way to the front. By nightfall on the 15th, the French had broken through and divided the armies of Wellington and Blücher, just as Napoleon had planned.

*

Wellington received the news of first contact at a ball that evening held in Brussels by the Duchess of Richmond. His response is well known: 'Napoleon has humbugged me, by God; he has gained twenty-four hours' march on me.'

His reaction was to mobilise immediately and move towards Quatre Bras, a strategic crossroads south of the capital. Then he went to bed. He was woken at 1.45 am by his Quartermaster General Sir William de Lancey, with the news that it was worse than they had thought and that Napoleon was actually beyond Charleroi.

✳

Napoleon, who himself had hardly slept, was informed at 6 am on the morning of the 16th that the Prussians had grouped at Sombreffe. He was pleased. This was far too far south. Too far from Wellington.

Napoleon rode to the village of Fleurus, and finding his intelligence to be correct, positioned his army to do battle with the Prussians and sent a message to Ney's left wing, which was advancing towards Wellington at Quatre Bras, to send d'Erlon's army corps across to help him defeat Blücher.

✳

Wellington meanwhile was concentrating on the crossroads and rode there, arriving at 10 am. He asked De Lancey for troop dispositions and was assured that the Reserve would be with him at midday and the rest of the army soon after.

In fact De Lancey was being somewhat being economical with the truth, and even as Wellington wrote a message to Blücher assuring him of his support, it must have been evident to his subordinate that such support would be impossible in the given time-frame. Unaware of this, Wellington rode across to a windmill near the village of Ligny to meet Blücher and assure him again in person of his support. Then he rode back to what there was of his own army, but not before commenting that Blücher was placing his men on a forward slope where they would be exposed to French gunfire and blown to pieces.

The stage was set for potential disaster.

2

16 June, 4 pm
Enghien, The Low Countries

The old road had never been intended for an army on the march. Nonetheless, for 500 years soldiers had trodden its path on their way to war. Now, in this hot midsummer of the fifteenth year of the nineteenth century, war had come here yet again. And yet again the road bore witness to an army. Redcoats this time, a long snake of them: infantry marching in column of threes and cavalry two abreast, twisting down through the low countries for mile after mile like a fresh red scar.

Horses and men jostled for space on the rutted road with carts, cannon, limbers and wagons, while scarlet-coated officers rode down the ranks, giving orders or simply shouting a brief hallo to old friends.

Trooper Sam Boulter, just turned twenty and longing for his native Suffolk, scratched at the itch in his armpit and cursed the lice that had made their home there and become constant companions to himself and his comrades. Giving up, he pushed a finger beneath his brass chinstrap, and scratching at the side of his head, wished that his regiment had adopted a less cumbersome and uncomfortable headdress.

Boulter was a dragoon. A red-coated 'heavy' cavalry-man. A big man, atop a big horse, armed with a razor-sharp

35-inch long sabre and a carbine. Dragoons were the shock troops of the British army. But Sam Boulter was no ordinary dragoon. He longed for one of the helmets worn by the two other regiments in his brigade – the Inniskillings or the Royals. Instead, he and his fellow troopers had to put up with this infernal thing, an 18-inch high fur cap with a gilt front plate above its shiny leather peak, and the white horse of Hanover galloping on the reverse of the crown. It was unique in the British army and marked out his regiment as something special, not that there was any need to tell Boulter that.

For 150 years, since their formation, the 2nd Royal North British, Dragoons had been known as the Scots Greys, on account of the fact that Scotland had been their country of origin and that they all rode, to a man, on grey horses. They made an impressive spectacle, and there was no unit to match their appearance in all the world. That at least was Boulter's opinion, even though at that moment he felt something less than noble.

He scratched again at his scalp and the headdress wobbled unnervingly. The bearskins were devilish hard to keep straight and horribly hot in summer months such as this. Worst of all, though, the thick fur of the bearskin was a haven for lice and all manner of crawling beasts. When wet it became matted and you could never get the damn thing clean. Of course the regiment had been issued with black oilskin covers, which all save the officers now wore while on campaign. But Boulter reckoned the thing was more use to the beasts, keeping them warm in the fur.

Giving up with his scratching, Boulter turned to his

left-hand man, William Dick from Paisley, and asked him how long he reckoned they had left to march.

Dick shrugged. He had no idea, and if the truth were known he was beginning to wonder if the General did. How much further was he going to make them go in a day? He spat out the wad of tobacco on which he had been chewing.

Boulter reckoned they had gone more than twenty miles since daybreak. They had come down the road from the Flanders town of Denderhauten, which had been their billet these past few weeks. Before that they had been in Ostend, and then back in Canterbury.

In Boulter's mind they were here for one reason. 'Boney' was out there and they had been sent to find him. And to send him packing and finish him off once and for all.

That was why they had come here. And why they were marching down towards France. To finish Napoleon. The great thief of Europe had slipped his chains on the isle of Elba, and in a matter of months had swept through France and back into power, raising a huge army and threatening once again to plunge Europe into another twenty years of bloody war.

But Boney, they knew, had stolen a march on them. Wasn't that what the Regimental Sergeant Major had told them? Napoleon was over the border from France. Had crossed at Charleroi. And now the Duke, old Nosey, Wellington himself, was taking them off down this damned road to beat the tyrant and send him back to hell. But he'd been wrong-footed. And so now they were chasing shadows.

Sam had faith on the Duke. Didn't they all? The hero of Spain and Portugal. But he had not fought under him before. They had not been in Spain, not the Greys. They were too precious by far. The Prince Regent, fat George, wanted them kept at home. And so they had spent the last ten years on parade, forever being inspected by foreign royalty: Germans, Russians, Dutch. There was no doubt they would be the best turned-out regiment on the field of battle. But could they fight?

Boulter knew they could. Not a few of them had come in from other regiments where they had seen service. But he himself had never killed a man. Nor had he ever even tried. Now he wondered what it felt like and if he could manage it. He supposed that when it came to it, it would be a matter of kill or be killed. Then you'd know.

A noise jolted him from his reveries and he turned back to Bill Dick. Like many of them in the Greys Bill had been a weaver by trade, in the mills at Paisley. But the problem was that there had been no trade and so he had enlisted in 1800, five years before Boulter had done the same, in the year of Trafalgar. But Dick had been in the fencibles before that. He was handy with a sabre and Boulter was thankful that they rode together in the line and would be together in the fight, when it came. He was a handsome fellow too, thought Boulter, one for the ladies, alright.

There was a booming sound against the sky, like distant thunder. Guns. But were they Wellington's guns or Boney's?

An NCO rode up, Troop Sergeant Major John Weir, an ex-shoemaker from Ayrshire. Weir had served seventeen years in the regiment, but in all that time had never seen a shot fired in anger. Not that you'd know it. His temper was fierce enough. A man of God, was Weir. He feared none but the Almighty, and everyone feared him. Perhaps, thought Boulter, that was why they had put him in charge of the regiment's funds. He growled at Boulter and Dick and ordered them to ride faster. The guns, he said, wouldn't wait. And nor would the Captain.

Boulter asked where they were, and was told that it was a place called Enghien on the road to Nivelles. And the sooner they got there the better.

You must be joking, thought Boulter. What the devil difference did Weir think spurs would make in a crowd like this? What did he want them to do? Leave the bloody column and go riding across country? Were they to go steeplechasing after Boney? Most likely he had had a tongue-lashing from the Adjutant – getting a dressing-down from Lieutenant Macmillan was not something anyone would relish.

Still, they had to move at the same pace as the rest of the army.

Besides, Boulter knew that he wouldn't keep Captain Fenton waiting. Fenton was a good man. Solid and experienced too. A rare thing among officers of the Greys, he was an Englishman. From Yorkshire.

He'd served in Spain, had the Captain, with old Nosey. Talavera and Salamanca. In the light dragoons before transferring to the Greys. Fenton was a good man, which was more than you might say for Mister Graham, their young lieutenant. In truth he was hardly a man at all, just 15 years old. An Englishman too, like the Captain, but that was where the resemblance ended.

Boulter watched the youngster now as they attempted

to hurry along the crowded, rutted road. Sergeant Swann was with him, had taken the lad under his care and Boulter knew that he'd promised the Captain to look out for him. He'd need to in the coming fight. It wasn't Swann the lad needed, he thought, it was a wet nurse.

He heard Weir's voice again, urging the men on. Thinking it might have an effect and wondering if there was any way through the mob, Boulter and his companion, not wanting to be left behind, dug their steel spurs into the flanks of their horses and the animals increased their speed, keeping up with the others in front of them and pushing with difficulty past the infantry around them. Who, he wondered, had chosen this bloody road?

＊

Twenty yards down the column, the same thought crossed the mind of Lieutenant Francis Stupart as he spurred into the flanks of his mare, a lovely 15-hander named Bessie, and struggled to push past a battalion of the German Legion. Who cursed him for his trouble.

A narrow road. It wouldn't do. And he said as much to the Sergeant Major, Alex Dingwell. Then he asked him where they were, and had the same answer as Boulter. This was Enghien, and Dingwell knew this to be true. He had heard it from the Adjutant.

Enghien. It meant little to Stupart. He knew it was south of Nivelles and closer to France. He had been with the regiment seven years. Had joined as a Cornet by purchase. Clackmannan was his home, though truth to tell, this was his home now. Anywhere the regiment was, that was his family.

He looked around him. It seemed as though the larger part of the army were attempting to move south-east through this little town. Carts and wagons and guns were everywhere. The enemy himself could not have slowed them better.

The sound of cannon-fire thrummed the air. It was quite distinct now, and from the direction in which they all seemed to be heading.

Major Cheney was ahead of them and Stupart spurred on a little to find him. Perhaps the Major would know where they were bound. But Cheney merely smiled at him and told him that Braine-le-Comte was their destination in the orders, twelve miles away south-east.

Towards the guns, he thought. And he was right.

They passed by Nivelles, where the road became more of a cart-track. The evening was coming in now and they rode towards the crossroads at Quatre Bras with the setting sun to their rear. They had not gone more than five miles since their last halt on the march, the road being flanked by woods on both sides, when they began to meet men coming the other way. Boulter looked at them. Wounded. They travelled on wagons and litters, but most of them were walking. Men with bandaged arms and heads. Some helping comrades. All of them grim-faced.

They came to a halt. Boulter turned to the Sergeant Major and inquired as to the delay. It was a wagon, which had lost a wheel a mile or so up ahead.

Looking down to his immediate left, Boulter saw a man with his arm in a sling. A Highlander, Black Watch from his dark green and blue kilt. The man stared at him, then recognised his tall, bearskin head-dress as belonging to the Scots Greys. Soon they were chatting, two men in two Scottish regiments in the same army talking of home. Boulter asked him about the French. The Highlander looked downcast. Oh yes, they had seen the French right enough. And they wouldn't forget it in a hurry. But it had been touch and go.

They thought they were going to win for their '*Empereur*'. They wouldn't give up easily. He looked at Boulter, aware of his accent, that he wasn't a Scot. Boulter told him of his home in Suffolk, Stowmarket. He explained that there were all sorts of them in the Greys, not just Scots but Englishmen and Irish too.

Then it came, the question he had been expecting. Weren't they band-box soldiers? Hadn't ever seen a fight, had they?

Boulter shook his head and tried to hide his anger, but explained that many of them had served in other regiments before joining the Greys. And all of them were ailing for a fight.

That seemed to satisfy the Highlander, who laughed and shook his head, muttering that they would be sick of it soon enough when the Frenchies stood their ground. But he wished them luck before going on his way to the rear.

The wagon had been moved now and Boulter trotted on, leaving the Highlander to walk on, nursing his mangled hand.

Soon enough, he thought. The Jock was right there. They would know their own mettle soon enough.

3

16 June, 5 pm
Near Quatre Bras

Riding a hundred yards or so in front of Boulter, at the head of Captain Vernor's troop, F troop of No. 2 squadron, Royal North British Dragoons, Cornet Francis Charlton Kinchant adjusted his seat on his grey mare, Dorothy, and wondered at the scene around him.

They had been in the saddle for some hours now, since dawn, give or take a few halts on the march. And it seemed to Kinchant that last night, the 15th of June, was now an eternity away. He and his fellow junior officer of the troop, Lieutenant John Mills, eleven years his senior, had gone to bed in the insalubrious farmhouse that had furnished their billet at about twelve o'clock. Both young men had felt slighted not to have been invited to attend the grand ball being held by the Duchess of Richmond in Brussels that night. It was said that the prettiest girls in Brussels, certainly all the English roses, were to be in attendance. Instead they had drowned their sorrows in a bottle of brandy that Mills had discovered in the house, and had been scarcely asleep when at two in the morning the trumpeter had sounded 'to horse'.

It was enough though to rouse their addled heads. In an instant both officers were out of bed, their small clothes, barely dry, removed from the washtub.

Cornet Lemuel Shuldham, Kinchant's great friend and, at 21, almost his exact contemporary, had arrived in the doorway before either man had been fully dressed. He was more animated than Kinchant had ever seen him, his face aglow with excitement. This was it, he told them. The French were across the border, at Charleroi, engaging the Prussians. Wellington had received news of it last night, at the Duchess's ball.

Kinchant had sneered. At the Duchess's ball! Good God, he thought, was everyone at the Duchess's ball? He asked Shuldham if he had been there, hoping for a reply to the negative. As he finished fastening his tightly fitted tunic, and began to buckle on his sword-belt, Shuldham replied that he had not attended, as no one from their regiment had been invited. It had been all Light Dragoons, Lord Uxbridge's favourites, Grant's and Vivian's men. None of the Greys' officers, nor those of the Inniskillings, nor even the Royals. Not even Colonel Hamilton had been on the guest-list.

It had not, he was assured, been much of an affair. But that had been where the news was received. A Prussian officer had brought it, covered in mud, straight from the battle. Boney had crossed the border and they were to meet him.

Shuldham, ever the clown, had placed his undress bicorne on his head, sideways, aping Bonaparte's own famous headgear. Then he had bent his knees and shoved his hand inside his coat.

Kinchant, picking up a crust of bread from their uncleared supper, threw it at him with an oath and the three of them had tumbled, laughing, out of the house and into the lane, Shuldham hastening off to rejoin his own troop.

They found Troop Sergeant Major Macmillan awaiting them. Macmillan, an ex-painter and decorator from Edinburgh and at five foot seven one of the shorter men in the troop, made up for his lack of inches in the strength of his arms and a dourly intimidating countenance. He greeted them with a polite 'Good morning, gentlemen'. Then looked hard at Mills. and told him with relish that the troop was assembled and Captain Vernor was awaiting him.

There was no moon and the troop had mustered in darkness, lit only by the orange glow from the camp fires which still burned from the previous evening.

Mills and Kinchant walked smartly across to where Vernor was waiting, sheathed sabres supported in their left hands, their bearskin caps tucked under their right arms.

Vernor spoke. 'Orders gentlemen. From Brigade. We are to concentrate on Ninove.'

He caught their glances, looking to gauge their surprise, then continued, saying that he didn't understand it. Ninove was north of them, and their intelligence suggested that Bonaparte had crossed to the south east, at Charleroi.

He paused and staring at the two officers, furrowed his brow and spoke to Mills. The Lieutenant had turned out without his gauntlets, and in Vernor's mind the man was in a state of undress.

Mills gazed down at his bare hands and then at Kinchant's hands, encased in the thick white leather gloves that were obligatory for all officers.

Vernor shook his head and muttered. It wouldn't do. Who could say? They might have a visit from General Ponsonby. Or Lord Uxbridge, or even the Peer himself.

He turned to the assembled men, who had fallen in, in three ranks. The four sergeants, four corporals and sixty-one private soldiers who made up his troop, Vernor's troop, his immediate family. He addressed them.

'Men, the French have moved this morning and we shall do so soon enough, but we have little real intelligence. I intend to make certain that when we do move we are moving in the correct direction. Now get to it. Carry on, Sar'nt Major.'

Troop Sergeant Major Macmillan barked at them to get themselves fed and the horses too.

Kinchant looked at them as they doubled about their business. He was in no doubt that his regiment was the finest in Europe, and of it, his troop the best. The men were, almost to a man, over five feet eleven in height. Giants, all of them. His fellow officers, the Captain and Mills, along with the others of the regiment, were fine gentlemen, though it struck him as odd that they should only number three Scots among them, the others all being English.

Kinchant himself was the son of a man of the cloth. His family, descended from Huguenots who had fought under Marlborough, had a parsonage, at the village of Easton, in Herefordshire, in the Welsh marches, and Francis had purchased his cornetcy this past January, just as soon as he was able to do so, a month past his 20th birthday. He wanted to see something of the world, to improve his position in a way that would not be possible at home. Besides, what was a parson's living?

The cavalry was his way out from a domestic hell, his passport to the world. But what, he wondered, had he seen of the world to date?

They had embarked at Gravesend on 15 April, reaching Ostend three days later. From there they had gone to Ghent, and by the beginning of May found themselves in Denderhauten, by Grammont. He had had his fill of the Low Countries, and could not offer much of an opinion of them save that they were in general very filthy.

His billet was small and smelly and much like a pigsty. The men and women of the country he found very plain, with mouths that reached from ear to ear, and they were also extremely ignorant. Few could speak French as well as he himself, and nothing but Flemish was spoken among the lower classes.

Kinchant's soldier servant Sam Kenmuir approached and he asked him his opinion of the locals. Kenmuir shook his head. There had been a pretty girl in Denderhauten, but mostly they were 'pokey wee folk', with 'right dreich' faces.

The man, ever resourceful, pressed a warm canteen of tea into Kinchant's hand.

As Vernor nursed his jaw and sent an orderly to the Colonel to make sure the bizarre orders were correct, the troop made ready, the men tightening their girths and adjusting kit, the officers ensuring it was smartly done, although in truth it was the troopers who were the old hands.

Kinchant meanwhile drank the tea and contemplated his finances. He had heard nothing from his father, the 'old man' as he called him, though he had sent to him for a further advance this last week. It had not been the first time. As soon as they had received orders to sail for Flanders, Kinchant, as ever lacking in funds, had written to his father:

'I shall have to purchase many essential though expensive articles, such as tent and tent equipage, &c., and many other things necessary for service. Our dress altogether is extremely rich and consequently costs lots of money. The Court dress coat alone is forty guineas. It is covered with lace from head to foot. The jackets are handsome. Every other part of the equipment is equally as expensive . . .'

Of course, he had had to borrow the necessary funds from his friends in the regiment, and prayed that every day would bring the much-needed covering notes.

Campaigning was a dashed expensive business. It had taken them seven days to march across England from Bristol to Gravesend. Mess bills every night, and his last bills from London still unpaid. He had had to acquire camp equipage, and the tradesmen were continually dunning for their accounts to be settled. And he did not expect to receive any pay for four months.

He was also concerned about his horse. She was just as short as she ever was. Too low for him by two inches, at least. The Colonel had passed her as a second charger, but he had expressed a desire that Kinchant should get one much stronger and higher immediately, as a first charger. But where, he wondered, was he to find a horse of that description?'

He had purchased a horse in London, but he had been gulled. The damn thing had gone lame. So Kinchant had bought another horse from Easton. She was a very promising animal, but rather too slight for his weight. He had lent her to Kenmuir. who he knew at least would treat her properly. He would just have to make do with what he had.

Mills had flattered him, saying that he was a match for any of them. But Kinchant knew that he was not a natural horseman, and had worked hard while the regiment had been at Bristol that spring to improve his riding, rising every morning at six to attend the regimental riding school till nine. In fact, he and Shuldham had gone there together, and had improved alongside one another as their friendship grew.

It was a little different to the method of country squires, which he had been taught as a boy. They rode without stirrups, in order to obtain a firm seat, leaping the bar and any number of ditches and going through all the different evolutions of field exercises. It had been worth it. Worth all the falls and bruises. Kinchant had known full well that when they did receive their posting for active service, only those with real skills at horsemanship in the field would go, and the others would be left behind in the home service squadrons. And he had been right. He thanked God that he had made it through.

It had been Sergeant Ewart's advice that he had followed. As always. Ewart had taken a real liking to him from the start, and he was ever thankful for it. For without Ewart's guidance, Kinchant thought, he should now be languishing in some English barracks, spending his days on parades and his evenings playing cards. But he knew he was hardly the equal of the Colonel, or Ewart, even though, as Mills put it, he could ride without stirrups 'like some Jintoo'.

So much for horsemanship. It was swordsmanship that he'd need when they met the French. And in that too, Ewart had taught him all he knew. All the moves.

He would need them. Sar'nt Major Macmillan had said that there would be more hard fighting and more bloodshed here than in any war any of them had yet seen. Boney was going to dispute every inch of ground with the sword.

He wondered, though, as the others did, what Bonaparte was doing at Charleroi? The clever thing to do surely would have been to have struck to the left, and cut their communications with the coast. But of course, what Boney did was anyone's guess. That's what had made him the terror of Europe. Hadn't his mother used to sing him a song about Bonaparte when he was a boy? Told him that if he wasn't good, Boney would come for him. He had been the monster of all their lives. Even Mills, older as he was than Kinchant, had admitted to having had dreams about him.

*

Eventually the orderly returned with an answer to Vernor's query as to their movement order. He had been quite right. Ninove was not their goal, but rather Quatre Bras, a crossroads on the Mons-Brussels road. A place where, if possible, Wellington might hold back Bonaparte. And so they had begun their march, and now here they were as dusk came on.

Again Kinchant wondered how much further they might go that day, and whether they would meet the French. Night was falling fast and then, abruptly, as if by order, the cannon ceased. He wondered what sort of supper they might look forward to. He recalled the great dinner they had held just before they had left Denderhauten for the 46 non-commissioned officers who had recently been promoted from the ranks. It had been a magical affair, with candles and lamps hung from the trees of an orchard and tables laid out below the trees. The thought again reminded him that they had missed the Duchess's ball and it irked him. Part of his plan in soldiering was to gain favour at court, and here had been an opportunity wasted. He had thought that a regiment renowned for its parades and fine dress must have the eye of the king, but perhaps he had been mistaken.

After the battle they would see. When he returned home a hero, then would come his chance.

*

A distant booming had been increasing in volume for some time, and now seemed close. Cannon-fire. Getting nearer.

Hardly had the thought left him, than the Duke himself came into view, riding in the opposite direction with his army. He spoke a word to Vernor and doffed his hat to Mills and Kinchant before passing on, escorted by a troop of the Blues. And they too carried on, pushing on the other way, towards the crossroads. So that was to be their role. No battlefield glory today, but the duty of a rearguard.

Up ahead, however, even though the Duke might have left the place, the battle was still raging. And suddenly they were a part of it. The wounded were among them now. Men – or rather the ruins of men. Men with parts of them blown away, yet somehow still walking or even crawling along the road. Others lay in jolting wagons, maimed and blinded, or were carried by comrades on planks and broken doors.

And then there were the dead, lying by the roadside, curled up like sleeping babies. Lifeless corpses. He gazed at them in wonder. For, unlike their wounded comrades, so many of them seemed not to bear a scratch.

And then a sudden curse jolted him from his reverie. To his left, pushed to the side of the narrow, rutted road, a cart containing wounded had hit a rock, and one of the soldiers, an infantryman in scarlet and grey, had tumbled off. Now, unable to use his bandage-swathed right arm, he clambered clumsily back on board, his comrades heaving him up, to continue on their way to Brussels.

Kinchant turned towards them, and as he did so, the man caught his eye and in that instant any remaining thoughts of court levees and royal favour left the young officer. For the man's eyes had caught him in their gaze, and within them he could see only one emotion. It was a look of pure terror.

4

Situation Report
Evening, 16 June

It had been a day of disasters. At Ligny, Blücher had been defeated by Napoleon and pushed back in retreat, losing 15,000 men. The battle had started at 2 pm and the fighting was bloody and often at close quarters, almost medieval in character.

Napoleon had waited all day for d'Erlon to arrive according to his order to Ney, but instead the General spent the day countermarching after continually being given conflicting orders by the mercurial Marshal. By nightfall the French had won, but it was not a death-blow, and Blücher retreated towards Wavre.

Infuriated with Ney, Napoleon decided to turn on Wellington and sent Grouchy with 30,000 men to pursue Blücher and prevent the two armies joining.

*

Meanwhile, at Quatre Bras, Ney had met Wellington but had failed to win a victory. The crossroads had initially been held by a division of Dutch Belgians. Most of them had been in French uniform and French service until recently, and in fact the only real change had been to their shakos. Wellington was not sure if he could trust them or their Francophile commanders. One of these, General

Perponcher, had orders that unless supported he should retire if attacked. But he deliberately disobeyed them. It was to be Wellington's salvation, for had the Dutch retreated, Ney might well have broken through. As it was, Wellington was now swift to take steps to use the Dutch Belgians' disobedience to his advantage.

Ney began his attack at 2 pm, outnumbering the Dutch Belgians by two to one. But an hour later the British Reserve, with Picton's 5th division of veterans including the three battalions of Highlanders, arriving on the field. Wellington, the master of concealment, hid the bulk of his men in the dead ground behind the crossroads.

Ney waited in vain for d'Erlon's corps, and ordered futile attacks throughout the day until, by 5 pm, Wellington outnumbered him and the battle ended in stalemate as the light faded. By the end of the day, the Allies had lost almost 5,000 men and the French 4,000.

5

16 June, 6 pm
Quatre Bras

The guns were louder now. Ahead of Francis Kinchant, riding at the very head of the column, leading all six of his troops, as it approached the crossroads, Lieutenant Colonel James Inglis Hamilton, officer commanding the 2nd, Royal North British, Dragoons, patted his well turned-out hunter and, leaning forward, whispered softly in her ear. His horse, he knew, had sensed that something was afoot. She was an old war horse, Irish-bred, fine over fences and hedges and as good as he had ever had under him.

Looking up he saw, directly before him, and riding in his direction, the figure of General Sir William Ponsonby, his Brigade commander, whose Union Brigade of heavy cavalry comprised the Greys along with the Irish Inniskilling Dragoons and the English Royal Dragoons, hence its title.

Ponsonby greeted him as an old friend. They were all assembling now. General Grant with his hussars, Somerset too with the Household Cavalry. He took up with Hamilton, and together they rode to find Lord Uxbridge, the cavalry commander, intent on discovering what they could of his dispositions.

They rode towards the large, high-walled farm which marked the crossroads and the small village to which it gave its name, Les Quatre Bras. The place was awash with wounded and among them were mounted staff officers. Seeing them approach, one of these, a hussar in the blue coat and bright red shako of the 7th, rode towards them. Hamilton recognised him as one of Uxbridge's aides.

The young man reined in and informed them that the brigade was to bivouac almost exactly where they were, forward of the farm.

Ponsonby nodded and asked at what stage they might be permitted to pursue the enemy. But the aide informed him succinctly that, as the French were not in retreat, there was to be no pursuit that evening.

Ponsonby turned to his right and gazed out at the battlefield. The fighting appeared to have ceased, or at least there was no sign of any melee or firefight. The cannon were still loosing off rounds. But nothing more. In the distance it was possible to make out the French and in the dusk the light of campfires.

No pursuit. They were to bivouac. Marshal Ney, it would seem, had not been beaten. And nor, mind you had they. Perhaps, he wondered, they might continue the fight tomorrow.

Then, off to find the remainder of his brigade, Ponsonby took his leave of Hamilton and the others.

✳

The regiment had dismounted now and Hamilton watched as the well-rehearsed routine began to take over. His men became occupied in doing what they could to find fodder for the horses, before seeking out their own food.

Among them were Sam Boulter and his friend William Bryce, a collier from Bo'ness. Close to the farm, although across the main road from where the colonel sat, both men dismounted, and turning from the saddle, Boulter drew back, suddenly startled by a face staring up at him in the moonlight.

The man was dead; his arm had been severed at the shoulder. Boulter looked at him and saw from his uniform he was a Belgian, dressed in French blue but with the Dutch lion on his buttons. Boulter grabbed one of them and pulled hard. It came away and he looked at it and wondered if changing the buttons on your coat could change the way you thought or the reason you fought. He hoped so, for these were the men alongside whom they would soon have to fight. A few months back these men had been fighting for Boney. All that had changed was their uniform. In fact the coat might have been a French one. His hat was different, mind you. It had two peaks – one back and one front.

Boulter remarked on it to Bryce, who told him the hat was of made in Austria. One thing was for certain, he thought. If they did refuse to fight or cut and run and flee the battlefield, wearing a hat with two peaks, they wouldn't be able to tell if you were coming or going.

*

The horses seemed content enough, despite all the death that lay around them. Boulter patted Mary, the fifteen-hand dapple-grey he had doted on these past four years. He had slung a feed-bag around her head and watched as she munched on some of the hay that they all carried in the string panniers they wore slung across their saddles.

Quiet though she was, he could tell that she was fair done in. Fifty miles they had come today, he reckoned, no less. He began to think of finding a bed for the night.

But there was to be no rest for Boulter quite yet. Bryce nudged him and pointed at a figure walking towards them.

Sergeant Hayward always seemed to be smiling, but God knew why, for whenever he appeared it was merely to issue a new order and tonight was no different. Before they had time to think, he had told Bryce and Boulter to form a foraging party. Eight men.

Moving quickly, the two troopers found six more men from their troop, and with oaths and curses, began to search for any form of provisions. Walking towards a farmhouse they found an encampment of feather-bonneted, kilted Highlanders gathered around a fire and, eager to hear any account, began to ask them about the battle. And then as quickly wished that they had not.

*

Close to where Boulter and Bryce had made their biv-ouac for the night, among the men of Vernor's troop in a field of clover, Francis Kinchant patted the flank of his horse and watched as she snuffled in the canvas nose-bag looped over her head. Their poor mounts had been exhausted after the fifty-mile march, but the baggage had been left behind and there was no fodder expect the little kept in their saddle-bags. He cursed the quartermaster and thought how typical it was of army life.

Like Boulter, Kinchant had been sent to forage. As

always, the Adjutant had selected an officer for the patrol and tonight it was Kinchant's turn.

The Adjutant, Lieutenant Macmillan, was one of the old hands of the regiment. Still a Lieutenant, although now in his 45th year, he had joined it in '86 and served in Flanders three times, rising through the ranks.

'You may encounter Prussians,' he had told Kinchant. 'How is your German?'

Kinchant said he had none.

'Well, that's too bad,' Macmillan had told him. 'You shall have to do what you can. Just make sure your pickets don't shoot them. Remember, they wear blue, like the French. And the Dutch.'

Kinchant had led a foraging party of men from his troop a short distance off on the road to Nivelles, where to the west they found a village, or what remained of one, for it had been so ravaged and plundered by an army, or perhaps more than one, that it seemed as if the hand of some great giant had picked up the houses and their contents and simply thrown them back down. With four of his men, Kinchant picked his way through the debris, thankful that he was not wearing the high, thigh-length boots which were full-dress for an officer and instead was clad in the same grey overall trousers and short boots as his men.

One of the men, Private Craig, shouted across to him that he had found lots of firewood, and Kinchant had reminded him that it was fodder, not firewood, they were after.

He became aware that there were others searching through the ruined village. Dim shapes in the evening light, they might have been from any regiment or any army, and for a nervous moment, Kinchant wondered if they might be the enemy, until one of them drew closer to him and spoke,

'Scots Greys, Sir?'

The voice was lilting, soft and Hebridean, and as Kinchant looked he could see quite clearly that the man was wearing a kilt, a Highlander.

'That's us. Who are you?'

'Black Watch, Sir. Forty-twa.'

'You were in action today?' Kinchant was eager to hear something of the battle.

The man nodded, and as he did so a number of his regiment gathered about him.

'Hard going, Sir. Damn hard.'

They were joined quickly by Kinchant's men. The young cornet leaned forward, 'You say the French fought well?'

The man nodded again, and another Highlander chimed in: 'Aye, Sir. They fought like the very divil.'

Kinchant asked him how it was they had neither won nor lost.

'Hard to say, Sir,' the Highlander replied, 'though I thought we were winning. The Frenchies seemed right beat back. They lost the wood and both the farms too.'

Then, rather cheekily, he added, 'We thought that your men might chase them up. You on your fine grey horses an a', Sir.'

Half of their battalion had been made casualties, and their Colonel killed. It had been lancers that had done for them. Not the red ones, nor the Poles, but the men in green, with gold helmets. They had come on again and again. Had broken the square.

One man in particular now caught his eye and maintained the stare. He was a sergeant of the same regiment with a cut on his cheek from the tip of a sabre. He had, he told Kinchant, been lucky. They had had Brunswick hussars at their flank to cover them but they had been untried. And when they should have charged to beat off the lancers and cuirassiers, they had retired.

The Dutch cavalry had run away too, said one of the man's comrades. The British had performed well enough, the Rifles, the Guards. But where, he wondered, had their own cavalry been?

It was a dismal tale. All of it. Kinchant felt stunned, unable to comprehend that a British army had been anything less than wholly victorious. He felt dispirited, as though everything had been knocked out from him which earlier in the day had filled him with such pride.

The man told him he had fought eight years under the Duke, and had never known him lose. But he was of the opinion that if it hadn't been for Marshal Ney's own mistakes, that might have been the case this time. He added that his captain had told him of a whole division that had spent the whole day marching from one battle to another. From Napoleon to Ney and back again, and never fought once.

Kinchant had not heard of another battle. The Highlander told him that Bonaparte had spent the day fighting the Prussians and had beat them. Thirty miles to the east. With losses of 20,000.

*

Kinchant walked on, followed by the rest of the foraging party, and wondering all the while if they would really teach the French a lesson. He was amused at the same time that they had thought him, a Shropshire boy, to be a Scot.

Eventually, with some effort, they managed to find some provisions in the ruined village: a round of cheese, a few dried sausages, a loaf of bread, and better than all these, a half-dozen bottles of red wine and two large flagons of Hollands gin. Importantly, in one of the barns they found a good supply of hay that would sustain the horses. Kinchant was conscious that they were under express orders from the Peer himself that there should be no looting, on pain of death, and that any provender and supplies should be paid for. The place, though, was entirely deserted and, deciding that discretion might be employed in the present situation, he ordered the men to rejoin the troop.

Arriving back at the lines bearing their booty, they found Kenmuir tending the mounts. He ordered him to have them linked in column, saddled and bridled.

Kinchant emptied the water from his canteen and replaced it with a generous helping of the Hollands. He cut a chunk of the bread and then, taking one of the sausages, he left the men to it and went in search of Shuldham with their supper, wondering if they would find shelter or sleep the night in the lines with the horses.

As he was passing the larger farmhouse which stood by the crossroads, Kinchant saw, in the dimming light, a familiar figure sitting on a chair under the roof of an open barn. He called out to Shuldham that he had their supper.

Shuldham arose from the chair and walked across to him, his hand behind his back. Then he drew it out and revealed a copper pan in which sat an egg and something that looked like a kidney, a calf's kidney. One of the men had found it. They had been carving the place up for the last two hours. Wellington, contrary to his usual practice, seemed to be allowing it. Everything had been brought out to make fires: ploughs, harrows, chairs, tables, anything that would burn. And all the animals had been butchered, old sows, pigs, calves and cows.

Kinchant reached into his haversack and brought out the sausage, bread and wine. And, with a flourish, his canteen full of Hollands. The French might not be beaten, but at least he and his friend would dine like kings.

*

Only three hundred yards away from them, Quartermaster Sergeant John Bishop had not been so fortunate. Although his was the job of providing for the regiment, there was not to be the luxury of a calf's kidney for him, this miserable evening.

The weather, he thought, had blighted the campaign which, thus far, had been for them all the greatest of adventures. They had embarked in mid-April in huge vessels; his was called the *Fame*. He had wondered if it was a portent. Was that the outcome he was expecting from this battle?

Major Poole had gone on board with him. Acting Brevet Major, that was, and Cornet Westby, the young Irish lad, newly joined. Sergeant Major Russell was there, the bible-basher, and Sergeant Johnston, Corporal Stoddart and Buncle, their trumpeter.

The talk, of course, was all of wives and children left behind. Wellington had allowed some of the wives in

Spain, but was not doing the same in the Low Countries. Some of them were there on the quay, crying their eyes out, children clinging to their petticoats and aprons as they screamed their goodbyes to their husbands.

The next morning they had set sail and reached Ostend a few days later. As Quartermaster Sergeant, Bishop had the job of supervising the drawing of rations for one day – man and horse both. And then they had marched on Bruges.

The country was good, level as a bowling green, and filled with birdsong. And the locals had been hospitable with their food, and not least the good Hollands gin. And so it had remained until May when, brigaded under General Ponsonby, with the Royals and the Inniskillings, they had drawn ten days' rations and moved off into the country.

That's when what he now referred to as 'his unpleasantness' had occurred.

It was a piece of nonsense, that business with the tents. The Regimental Quartermaster had ordered him to collect equipment that lay in the street and account for it, but on returning they had been found to be short of four tents. He swore he had thought these been taken forward by the Troop Sergeant Majors, but when he had caught up with the rest of the regiment he discovered that they did not have them. And what had the bloody Quartermaster done? Only reported him to Colonel Hamilton.

The Colonel, for whom Bishop retained the utmost respect, had informed him in a matter-of-fact way that unless he could pay for the tents he would be tried by court martial. Well, he had no more money to pay for so many tents than the next man, and so there had been nothing for it but to accept the court martial instead.

Bloody court martial. Bishop had prepared his own defence, but it was days before the court eventually sat, on 7 May. What a day that had been. But he had done his best, argued his case and in the end he had been acquitted. After all, the tents had never been his to lose.

There had been promotions in the ranks after that, to bring the regiment up to field strength. No fewer than 15 new sergeants and 33 corporals had been added, and that had meant a right party. They had held it in an orchard and hung candles and lamps on the trees like a village wedding, setting up a banqueting table made with planks. What a night. They had drunk the health of King George without ceasing in brandy and wine, and then that of the Duke of Wellington and the Duke of York and Prince Blücher and anyone one else they could think of. His head had been heavy the next day, but he took consolation in the fact that, for a few hours at least, all his cares had gone.

It had been lucky that they had had some days to recover before the grand review. He recalled how Wellington had passed through their ranks, and with him old Blücher himself who stank of gin and had kept smiling and pointing out their horses and turnout. It had all seemed too good and just too easy.

But all that changed on the 16th. At two in the morning they had been woken by the trumpet call and shouts of 'to horse, to horse'. Within an hour they were making for the French frontier, to Nivelles. And it had been there that at last they heard the pop of distant musket fire.

And now they were sat here, twenty miles further on. Quatre Bras. What a stink-hole, thought Bishop. Opposite that same army.

He looked around at the place, lit up by bonfires. Shortly after they had got there, Bishop had been heartened by the sight of them, thinking they were intended to signal a victory. But instead he found they had been lit only to enable the surgeons to carry out their butchers' work and dress the wounds of the hundreds of wounded redcoats, Belgians and Brunswickers gathered at the crossroads in desolate groups. One of them had told him how their wounded commander being carried back to the rear had been attacked by a party of green-coated Lancers, and all of the party killed. He had been shocked. What sort of behaviour was this? Not that, most certainly, of the British soldier to a vanquished foe. He wondered what sort of men these Frenchies were to kill men in cold blood? And then of a sudden he felt weary beyond measure and wondered again where he was to spend the night.

6

16 June, 7 pm
Quatre Bras

Just fifteen minutes earlier, Colonel James Hamilton had asked himself the same question, but shortly afterwards he had made his own bivouac in a house a short distance behind the crossroads. It was one of the few on the road that had escaped the scavengers, and as so often before, he thought, he had been luckier than most.

Sitting now at the wooden table, his pencil poised over the small, open notebook in which he planned to make the day's report, as he had every day since first attaining the rank of Major in 1803, he paused and thought again on his extraordinary good fortune. How it had brought him thus far. He had not always been an officer and a gentleman, far less commander of the finest regiment of cavalry in the British army.

There were few in the regiment, indeed not many in the army, who would have guessed that the great Colonel James Inglis Hamilton, the very model of a Scottish gentleman, had been born into poverty in 1777, in North America at place called Ticonderoga in New York.

His mother had been a camp follower of the British army of King George as it had waged its war to retain the colonies for the Crown. His father, William, had been a mere sergeant major in the 21st foot, the Royal Scots

Fusiliers. Hamilton's name had been different then. He had been christened James Anderson, Jamie to his family. And for the first time, but not the last, fate had smiled on young Jamie.

After the American war, in which his father had been badly wounded, the family had returned to his father's home town of Glasgow, and there one day, while playing with his six children outside a tavern, the Saracen's Head, William had been spotted by the commander of his old regiment, Colonel Inglis Hamilton, by this time no less than a General. That had been the start of it all. The General had stopped his carriage and spoken to William. More than this, he had picked up young Jamie, then aged six, and tossed him up in the air. He could remember it even now. 'Do it again,' he had said to the old man. 'Again, again!' The General, who was himself unmarried and without children, had been captivated, and so had begun a great friendship. The General's visits to the family had increased in number, and at length he had expressed a desire to help with young Jamie's education. And so it was that not only he, but his brothers too, Willy and John, were given a privileged private education at Glasgow Grammar School and then at the city's great university. How many letters had the General sent to his 'Dear wee Jamie', he wondered. He had been the best scholar in the school. His three sisters too, Ann, Jean and little Grace, were educated at Glasgow's boarding schools. In addition James was taught to ride, and divided his time between his patron's country house, Murdiestoun, and his parents' humble dwelling in Glasgow's Gallowgate, opposite the tavern.

A military life was clearly meant for him, and the cavalry was the finest choice. When he was 15 years old, his adopted father had bought him a cornetcy in the Greys, the General's first regiment, his name on the letter of commission being James Inglis Hamilton. He was also given a generous allowance of two hundred pounds a year.

That had been 22 years ago, back in '93. He had fought in Flanders with the Duke of York, firmly believing that they would beat the French and send them home.

At Willems the following year they had charged and broken a French square, but the campaign had ended in ignominy. The young Cornet, on the other hand, had turned out well, being raised to Captain in '94 and Major in 1803. By 1807 he was Lieutenant Colonel of his regiment and still the old General's pride and joy, popular and beloved by his officers and men.

The General had made his will, leaving his property to James and his male heirs. At his funeral Jamie acted as chief mourner, accompanied by the nobility and gentry of the county. Afterwards he had bought a smart town house at York Street in Glasgow and settled money on his family.

It had been a charmed life indeed, and here he was now about to embark upon the most exciting episode yet. How he wished the General had lived to know it.

The Greys were his life. His love. Well, aside from his dear wife. He had met her while posted to Canterbury and they had married just last year, barely a year before he had been ordered to Belgium on the escape of Bonaparte.

He was a little concerned that the regiment had seen no action since the 1790s. They had not shared Wellington's glory in Spain, but had been kept by the King's specific orders in England – a showpiece, it was said in mockery, no more than toy soldiers, fit only for parades. Of course James knew better, but they had yet to prove it.

Regimental life had its many good points. James loved the ritual and the traditions, and their unique dress – the fact that they still wore the bearskin head-dress they had been awarded as a badge of honour after beating the French grenadiers at the battle of Ramillies in 1706, when they had fought under the great Duke of Marlborough.

He relished the fact that the officers never stood for the loyal toast. At first he had thought this treasonable, until told by one of the more senior majors that it dated back twenty years to '73 when old King George had received them while at Greenwich, and had himself been quite incapable of rising to reply to the toast.

All such things were meat and drink to James. Ten years ago now, they had formed part of Nelson's funeral cortège, and shortly afterwards James had been given command of the regiment. They had had a spell in Dublin, and by 1814 were back in Kent.

So now, after 20 long years, he and his regiment were to see action again. Their time was now. He knew it. Tomorrow would see great things. Something to go in the history books. Something to tell their children.

He wondered how his brother officers would fare. Only a bare handful remained of the old comrades who had fought the French in '94. The others were mostly rich young men who, though he was sure they might be brave enough when following a fox or in pursuit of the fairer sex at a ball, had never seen a Frenchman, let alone fought one face to face.

He wondered if he might be killed, or what was perhaps worse, end up like his dear brother John, maimed for life in Spain. John, a captain in the 21st, had fought at Salamanca. The French cavalry had caught him and cut him up, and now he was an invalid.

James hoped he would not suffer such a fate. He hoped too that soon his wife might bear him a child of his own, and yet he could not help but wonder if he would see his thirty-eighth birthday, in just two weeks' time.

The fire was dying in the grate, and as Hamilton picked up another log to cast upon it, an officer entered. Major Isaac Clarke had served in the Greys with Hamilton all through his career, having joined as a Cornet in 1795. They had been together in Flanders, and enjoyed the happy camaraderie of two brothers-in-arms.

Clarke told him that his servant, Callender, had managed to find them some supper. A ham. As he said the word the private entered, bearing in a pannier the fruits of his scavenging. There was ham, bread, sausage, a nice drop of Rhenish wine, a bottle of Hollands, a piece of cheese and some butter. Hamilton thanked the man and said that he presumed the food had not been looted.

Callender shook his head and smiled. Hamilton laughed. He took Callender for the finest servant any officer had ever had. The man, who was as tall as the colonel and four years his junior, could conjure food and wine from nowhere. He had only been with the Greys for two years, but Hamilton had selected him on instinct as successor to his previous servant, invalided out with rheumatics. Callender could polish boots till they shone like a mirror and always seemed to be on hand just when he was needed. He'd been a baker before, in Falkirk. In fact he was one of the celebrated 'Falkirk dozen' who were in the regiment – although, as he often reminded Hamilton, with him included it was really a proper baker's dozen, as there were in fact thirteen of them.

Callender set the table, and within a few minutes the interior of the cottage had been transformed and the two officers sat down to dine by the light of six candles, stuck in plates and mugs around the room. They had just finished their first glass of wine and a plate of sausage, when another man entered. The Adjutant, Henry Macmillan, had a nose for food.

With him came another officer, James Carruthers, a lieutenant. As they settled down to eat, Hamilton smiled to himself. Here they all were, the four of them, sharing the same food in the same circumstances, and yet beneath their uniforms they were, in their origins, as different as chalk and cheese.

Macmillan, a canny Fifer from Kirkcaldy, who had never lost his accent, was his elder by some six years. He had risen through the ranks to his present lieutenancy. Hamilton respected him, aware that they shared similarly humble beginnings. Carruthers, on the other hand, was the real thing, the scion of an ancient Scottish house who could rightfully claim to stem from the same line as no less than Robert the Bruce himself. At just twenty-one, he was the youngest man at the table and, despite his noble birth, among these men, heroes all to him, it was he who considered himself honoured.

As Callender poured the wine, the Colonel quizzed the adjutant, 'Henry, what news have you for us? Anything to report?'

'News is that Marshal Blücher is holding, Sir. Sent a message from Ligny. Just arrived. Took an hour to get to us, but they're holding the line. I just had it from Colonel Hervey and he from the Duke himself.'

Hamilton nodded. This must surely be true. Felton Hervey was the most loyal and reliable of men. An assistant quartermaster-general, he had lost his arm against French cavalry at Oporto and always ensured that he and his orderly were mounted upon English hunters, the better to ensure their escape from the enemy.

Macmillan stabbed at a piece of cheese and pushed it into his mouth while Hamilton considered the news. So, the Prussians were not beat. Wellington would be preparing to go on the offensive.

If Blücher could hold Bonaparte at Ligny, then there would be no reason why Wellington could not attack Ney here at Quatres Bras tomorrow. He was now his superior in numbers, and with themselves and the rest of the brigade, the Household Cavalry and the Light Dragoons, he would have all he needed.

He raised a glass. 'A toast. To tomorrow. And to Bonaparte. Even the most cunning of foxes cannot outwit a truly skilled huntsman.'

7

17 June, 8 am
Quatre Bras

Morning had broken over the battlefield of Les Quatre Bras and with it came a better idea of the full extent of the carnage that had taken place there on the previous day.

The fields, which before had been covered with waving corn, were now entirely trodden down and filled with the bodies of the dead and dying. A breathless silence lay over the place, punctuated by the low moaning of the wounded.

The dead, men and horses together, lay strewn in all manner of contortions and attitudes. And with them lay the detritus of war: artillery carriages, muskets, swords, pistols and cartridges, mixed with personal possessions, and everywhere papers and keepsakes were being blown about. Although the uniforms of the men showed a variety of colours, many of them had already been stripped by scavenging peasants. Even as the first rays of the sun came through, Sam Boulter, tightening the girth of his mount, watched the Provosts, mounted troopers of the Blues on their fine bay horses, riding down those who chose to chance death at their hands against the opportunity to make a quick fortune from robbing the dead. The Provosts showed no quarter and as Boulter watched he saw the flash of a pistol take the life of a peasant woman, who fell to join the thousands of dead killed in battle.

Boulter muttered to himself. This was a bloody business.

The sky above them was red and lowering, foretelling an approaching storm. The atmosphere too, the very air on this June day seemed oppressive and exhausting.

Boulter pulled again at the strap, and deciding it was secure enough, began to look for breakfast.

*

Colonel James Hamilton emerged from his billet and blinked in the daylight. But it had been the smell that hit him first. The acrid smell of gunpowder mixed with the cold freshness of the ground and the morning air, the smell from the cooking pots of 'stirabout' porridge into which all manner of food had been thrown, and above it all the unmistakable, sickly-sweet stench of death. Across the field he could see smoke rising from campfires of the allied army, and in the distance the same plumes rising from those of the French. So, he thought, they are still here. He had been nursing the impossible thought that during the night Ney might have given up and taken his army back to Paris. After all, hadn't he been abandoned, left short of reinforcements, by his blessed Emperor the previous day?

He walked down to the crossroads and surveyed the scene. The large farm had been turned into a field hospital and was still filled with the wounded and dying. Beyond it, on a small patch of bloody grass, lay hundreds of bodies piled up upon one another. Hamilton turned away.

The road to Brussels was filled already this morning with wagons commandeered from the farms and crammed with the badly wounded.

Hamilton wondered when he might expect orders from Ponsonby or Uxbridge. He presumed that the Duke was still biding his time, waiting for the moment. That was his way. Timing would be everything now.

He turned to his trumpeter, who had been waiting outside the cottage.

'Galstoun, be ready. I expect to be ordered forward at any time.'

The man nodded, grasped the brass trumpet and swung it down around his back where it hung by its gold and scarlet silken cord, and held it ready in his right hand, waiting for the signal.

But Hamilton's trumpeter was to have a long wait.

*

A little distance to the left and rear, Quartermaster Sergeant John Bishop shifted in his saddle and waited for the next command. The French had been up with the dawn. Bishop had spotted them. Skirmishers at first, moving in front of their infantry, pop popping with their muskets. But instead of the expected attack, none had come and at ten o'clock it seemed to Bishop that the French army could be seeing moving away.

The Brigade had been ordered forward, and he had thought they might pursue, but to Bishop's surprise, the orders when they came were to halt, and so here he had been standing for an hour and a half. At length, as Lieutenant Wyndham walked past, casting his eye over the state of their harness, Bishop had thought to ask if he knew what was afoot.

And Wyndham answered that it was a ruse. The Duke was showing what would appear to be an army to the French, the Greys and all the horse and artillery, while in fact he had taken away the rest of the army. The infantry had gone.

Bishop looked to their rear and saw nothing now but open fields, dotted with the occasional dead or wounded man. Wyndham was right, they had gone. The Duke, it seemed, was retreating.

*

It was not until a little after midday, however, that an officer finally rode up to Colonel Hamilton. Seeing the man approach, Hamilton looked up at the sky, which had become darker in the last few hours, with heavy, black clouds which Hamilton knew must become thunderous. Soon it would rain.

The approaching figure, Major Thomas Reignolds, Ponsonby's brigade major, was an old friend and trusted confidante of Hamilton's who had been seconded from their regiment and was in fact only some four years his own junior. But the news which he brought from the General was less than welcome.

The Greys were to form the third line of the rearguard and to retire on the village of Genappe. Hamilton paused a moment, bewildered, and asked Reignolds to repeat the order.

Yes, they were to retire on Genappe, up the Brussels road, covering the infantry; and thereafter they were to direct themselves towards the village of Waterloo at a place called Mont St Jean.

They were not to engage the French. Reignolds confirmed the news that Blücher's Prussians had been beaten and driven back on Wavre. It would be impossible for the Duke to hold at Quatre Bras without his help, and so the army was to retire in its entirety. The general orders were to fall back on Waterloo, and those for the Greys and the rest of the Union Brigade were to cover the withdrawal, along with all the cavalry.

Hamilton was aghast. Nevertheless an order was an order. He asked for more precise directions.

The cavalry was to form four lines. First the pickets, second the hussar brigade and some of the light dragoons, third the heavy dragoons, including the Greys, and lastly the bulk of the light dragoons. The Greys were to remain at the crossroads until the infantry had effected their escape.

Reignolds took his leave and Hamilton turned to his staff officers, a trio of whom hovered around. Firstly to a young cornet by the name of Edward Westby, who would deliver the order to Major Hankin and Captain Poole. Trotter was to find Captain Barnard and Captain Payne, and Shuldham, Captain Fenton and Captain Vernor.

Kinchant could not believe the news. Why the devil were they to retire?

Shuldham, who had come direct from Vernor, had the answer: Marshal Blücher had taken a licking and been driven back 15 miles. How could they stand without his help? Mont St Jean? Where the devil was that?'

Shuldham seemed to know. It was ground that by all

accounts had been previously selected by the Duke, on which to engage the French. Very favourable, he had been told.

The adjutant, Lieutenant Macmillan, rode past them at speed, shouting a command as he did so for the infantry to retire by the high road and the cavalry to form in line of divisions, from the left.

No sooner had the command been given than the heavens opened at last and the rain began to fall in torrents.

*

A French gun had unlimbered and was firing on the regiment, but had not yet made their range. John Bishop thanked God for that and prayed that the command to retire would reach them soon. As he did so a ball flew over their heads; his mount shook with fright and he held her tight lest she should panic. And, at the same time, the French infantry began to move towards them. A dense black mass of men. Unstoppable, it seemed.

To Bishop's left, Willy Mitchell spoke. 'Here they come, Sergeant. Like a plague of bloody locusts.'

There was a barked command from the Colonel, which neither man could hear above the cannon-fire, but then it was relayed by the Regimental Sergeant Major and Captain Poole's voice rang out, 'The troop will retire. Right wheel. At the trot.'

They went at a walk at first and then increased to a trot. They had left the ground to the rear of Quatre Bras now and entered a narrow cross-country road, full of holes and deep ruts which had filled up with the rain.

Bishop cursed. These were the worst possible of riding

conditions. The soil was stiff, slippery red clay and treacherous under hoof.

Slowly they made their way along the road, and from time to time a call would come from the rear exhorting them to quicken the pace. All around them men were jostling forward and slipping on the clay, being pushed into the ditch at the side along with horses and riders.

At last, and to Bishop's great relief, they came to the end of the road, some four miles away to the north from the crossroads. Now, perhaps, they would be able to make some ground away from the enemy. The country to the left would be fine, thought Bishop. A great, open plain. Perfect for cavalry.

Francis Kinchant found himself looking at the same ground, with the same thoughts. A small, inclining plain with a wide, open space to his left, perfect for cavalry manoeuvres. At that moment Colonel Hamilton came riding up and asked him the whereabouts of his squadron commander. Kinchant, much to his embarrassment, was not entirely sure.

Hamilton told him to find Captain Vernor, form the troop and hope that the squadron would follow suit. They were to about face and form up in line, facing the enemy, the squadron to form on them, using their position as its guide.

Hamilton, clearly in some agitation, rode away and Kinchant looked for Vernor, whom he found close by. He relayed the orders and Vernor, finding the Sergeant Major, put the men in column of twos.

Within a few minutes, the regiment had reformed precisely in accordance with Hamilton's instructions. The rain was coming down in torrents now, but Kinchant could see the French advancing towards them across the open fields. They halted less than half a mile away, and Kinchant watched in admiration coupled with apprehension as their horse artillery unlimbered quickly and smoothly. A few minutes later they opened up, and for the first time in his life he experienced the unpleasant sensation of being fired upon.

*

The roundshot began to fall in the ranks of the brigade. As Kinchant watched, a ball hit the ground and by some unhappy quirk of fate, in all that mud, chanced to hit a patch of more solid earth. It bounced up not unlike, he thought, a cricket ball, and hit the mount of one of the men in Captain Barnard's troop square in the chest with a ghastly thump, tearing a hole in the animal. At the same time her rider took the impact. The shot took off his right leg and he fell sideways off his saddle with a moan that became a scream. Kinchant stared in horror, and suddenly Ewart was at his side.

The big sergeant whispered some calming words and Kinchant felt instantly assured. It was always best, Ewart said, to keep your eyes to the front.

Kinchant looked round to his front and saw the French continuing to fire at them, the specks of black growing in size as they neared them to become recognisable as cannonballs. Most, luckily, flew over their heads.

Ewart saw that Kinchant's mind was still on the horror

he had witnessed. He spoke again and advised that they needed to charge them. They or someone had to. That would be the only way.

*

But it was not the Dragoons, though, who charged the French. In fact it was rather the other way. For as they watched, a regiment of green-coated French Chasseurs à Cheval, their sabres 'à point', came galloping up the road in column of assault and careened into the 11th Light Dragoons, who lay across it in line. The effect was like watching a breaker smash against a wall, bursting through the stonework as it came. Several of the British went down instantly, but then came the clash of sabre on sabre, the clang of metal as both sides went at it.

Gradually, however, Kinchant could see that the British were being pushed back. He turned to Ewart, and enquired as to what they should do.

But Ewart said nothing, for then, even as the Light Dragoons broke before them on the road, under the force of the Chasseurs, another regiment came forward from the rear to take their place, and at their head, resplendent in gold-trimmed shako and leopardskin saddle-cloth, rode Lord Uxbridge himself.

The horsemen behind him were redcoats this time, the Life Guards, and the French had seen them too. Suddenly the Chasseurs were seized with panic. They began to turn in all directions, anywhere to get away from the redcoated men in helmets on the big bay horses. But it was too late. The Household Cavalry crashed into them, and with unquenchable pride rising inside him Kinchant, almost cheering, watched as the foremost Chasseurs fell to the impact, while the others fled down the road back along the way they had come.

A cheer went up from the British cavalry. And as it did, with a terrible clap of thunder, the heavens opened again and this time with more ferocity than Kinchant had ever witnessed. It rained as if the water were tumbling out of tubs, and very soon their open meadow looked more like a lake.

From the rear of the troop some wag spoke above the thunderstorm. Something about not having enlisted for the marines. Kinchant smiled and hoped that the deluge would stop soon. Better to die in battle than to drown.

8

17 June, 2 pm
The Quatre Bras-Brussels Road

Despite his surprise at being told to stand and face the enemy, John Bishop was impressed and awed by the sight that now met his gaze. There behind them, not 500 yards distant, was what looked to him like the entire French army.

He turned to George Rennie, 'Christ. Will ye look at them!'

Musket shots came in, and at length one of them struck someone of the troop. Bishop looked to see who it was, but the man had fallen from his horse.

The French were on a hill now, and to his right he heard a shout as the British 7th Hussars, splendid in their scarlet shakos, charged towards a body of helmeted Lancers and Cuirassiers. For a moment the French looked as if they might waver, but they held their ground, and with a great crash the Hussars made contact.

It was bold gesture, thought Bishop, but no more than that, and very quickly, knowing they were beaten, the Hussars turned and retired to the lines.

Perhaps now, he thought, the Greys would be given the order to attack. But instead he watched as the Life Guards moved against the French cavalry.

He muttered under his breath. For God's sake. When

would it be their turn? But he knew that it would come soon enough.

As they looked on, the Life Guards slashed and hacked at the French cavalry, but after a few minutes, like the Hussars, even the Household Cavalry were beaten back.

As they were retiring a new sound came to him. A rattling with a distinctive beat. Drums. The French infantry on the move. Rennie spoke, told him that tune was 'Old Trousers'. 'Infantry, bloody infantry, that is.'

Scarcely had the words left his lips, than over the hill to the rear of the cuirassiers came a column of blue-coated infantry, their muskets raised high at the porte, bayonets glistening and in their midst a fluttering tricolour.

There was a boom to his left and Bishop saw cannon-balls coursing towards the French column, smashing into them and knocking down entire files like ninepins.

Now, he thought, surely they must attack.

He heard Poole's voice again. 'Scots Greys will retire. File from the right in half squadrons.'

Bishop shook his head – they were pulling out again. Today was not to be their day of glory.

Without a backward glance they made the road and found it choked with troops, all of them Allied and all of them heading for the same destination, a ridge line just to the south of a village named Waterloo.

*

It must have been close on 8 pm when Bishop at last admitted to himself that he was starving. And the smell of roasting pig was making his hunger worse.

Rennie was still with him. Had been all afternoon,

on the march north. All day they had talked of battle. But now the conversation had turned. The issue of the moment was, how much longer till their supper was cooked?

They had arrived here, their final destination, he presumed, some two hours ago, and had instantly set about making a fire. The farm to their rear had supplied the material. They had taken any stick of furniture that might be burnt.

And then had come the search for food. Eventually they had found a piglet, covered in mud in a corner of the yard. It was clearly the runt with little flesh to it, but it would have to do. They had slit its throat and skewered it, but neither man was convinced that it was cooked and neither wanted to be the first to try it.

The smell, though, had attracted visitors, and Bishop looked up to see two new faces in the firelight. An Irish voice broke the silence, asking if there was any spare for their fellow dragoons, the Inniskillings.

Rennie nodded, and invited the Irish to join them. There was enough to go round, if they had anything for the pot.

There was a commotion behind the two men and laughter, and they turned to see a party of kilted redcoats advancing towards them. A mixed bag – Black Watch, Gordons and Cameron Highlanders. They shouted a hallo. Glad to see another Scottish regiment and cavalry at that.

The Irishman asked the newcomers if they had anything to add to the pot, and from beneath his arm one of the Highlanders, a huge man, over six foot tall, drew a fat, squealing pig. He gazed down at the scrawny beast on the fire and laughed, before, with a quick movement, drawing his dirk from his stocking and slitting the animal's neck. Then quickly he cut it open, and pressing down on its back, pushed so that the entrails fell on to the ground, where he trod them into the mud. The carcass he threw on to the fire, skin and all.

The Irishman held out a cup of whiskey to him, Irish. The Highlander took a swig, and spoke of what might happen on the next day. That it was good to be among Scots and Irishmen. He told them that the kilted infantry would stop the French in their tracks, so that the horsemen could finish them off 'for old Nosey'.

After a while and more passes of the grog, they pulled the pig from the fire and without delay began to divide it up. Bishop's share was a foreleg and part of the head. It was not the finest food he had ever eaten, but it was hot and sweet, and with the whiskey and some brandy that another of the men had procured, it made a fine supper.

*

James Hamilton was not a man for rigid rules. Discipline, yes, when it was needed. He would enforce the law to the letter if needs be, and would flog his men where it was the right thing to do. But he knew too that on the eve of battle the men expected more of their officers, and so it was that the evening saw him wandering the lines, talking to them when he could.

Now, around a fire ahead, he spotted the Quartermaster Sergeant, along with a few others of the troop and men come in from other regiments. He liked Bishop and had been grieved when he had been reported for stealing. He had been equally pleased when they had found him not guilty.

Hamilton approached them, and as they did so, Bishop recognised him and stood to attention.

The others stood, murmuring deferentially.

Hamilton smiled, told them to stand easy and apologised for interrupting their eating. He looked at their grease-covered hands and tried to work out what their supper might be. The he saw the pig's ear in Bishop's hand.

Bishop was quick to assure him it had been got fair and square, from the Highlanders. Hamilton knew the Duke's obsession with plunder. He toyed with the Highlanders, not quite accusing them of stealing, but they knew it was on his mind. A shooting offence. In the end he laughed, and told them all to enjoy their supper, of which in truth he was quite envious.

He saw the bottles and cups, and asked what was in the beaker. The Inniskilling offered him some: 'Finest Irish, Sir.'

Hamilton accepted and, taking the mug, sniffed at the contents and then sipped at the whiskey. The straight spirit rasped on his throat and hit him with its warmth. It was not Scotch, of course, but it was still very fine. And very welcome on such a night as this. He thanked them all and then wrapped his cloak around his shoulders, even though he knew that, sodden as it was, it gave no further protection against the rain.

Hamilton looked at their faces in the firelight, as if to mark them on his mind, and began to wonder which of them might survive the coming battle. Then it dawned on him again that he himself might not. He shivered and took another sip. How many engagements had he been in? It was always the same on the eve of battle. Nervousness that gave way to good humour.

Hamilton took a last sip, drained the mug and handed it back to the Irishman, then turned to Bishop and wished him well.

As the Colonel strode away, the others smiled at one another. The Irishman, pouring out another shot, praised their Colonel and Bishop smiled with pride. It was true, Colonel Hamilton was in a class of his own. One of the better sort of officers. He would lead them well tomorrow. But Bishop knew in his heart that, however well he might lead them, it was all in the lap of the gods as to who would live and who would die. And who but they could know?

The Irishman shook his hand and made an oath. Whichever of them survived tomorrow, they would all of them meet up where they now stood at the Greys' camp, when it was all over. They muttered in agreement, and then Bishop spoke, correcting him. He pointed at the sky. They would not meet tomorrow after all. They would meet today. For the sun had begun to rise.

9

Situation Report
Morning, 17 June

The morning of the 17th was wet and unwelcoming, and at Quatre Bras, in between finding breakfast and discovering which of their friends still remained alive, both armies popped off a few shots at each other.

Wellington and his staff had stayed the night at the Inn of the Roi d'Espagne at Genappe, but had woken at five o'clock and ridden back to the crossroads. Amid the waking army there were dead and wounded lying everywhere.

Wellington had sent an aide, his old friend Alexander Gordon, to find Blücher, but Gordon found only the French and learnt from General Ziethen that the Prussians were falling back on Wavre.

In fact Gniesenau, suspicious of the British especially as their promised help had not come, was all for moving back towards Prussia, but was persuaded to make a less drastic move.

Had Blücher not pulled back, Wellington might have attacked the French. But now, isolated, he could not. He was forced to pull back from the crossroads, despite having not lost the battle.

Always, perhaps surprisingly, one step ahead, Wellington knew the terrain and had ridden it the year before, and De Lancey had a Royal Engineers' map, made during that recce, in his valise.

Wellington had marked on the map a line ten miles north, along a ridge with a chateau, three farms and some houses at a crossroads. That was where they would stand, and that was where they would wait for the Prussians.

The position at the ridge of Mont St Jean allowed him to hide his army on a reverse slope, just as he had done at Bussaco. But better still, to his front he had three strongpoints, the chateau of Hougoumont in the west, the farm of La Haye Sainte in the centre, and the combination of Papelotte farm, the chateau of Frichermont and the farm of La Haye in the east.

The crossroads at the ridge was also a confluence of roads from Blücher's position, and was backed up by a system of lateral roads which suited his mobile defence system perfectly.

It was, in short, the perfect defensive position. But, if Blücher did not come, then Wellington knew that he would have to retreat and abandon Brussels to the French.

*

Napoleon arrived at Quatre Bras at 2.30 pm, just as the British rearguard were pulling out. He personally pursued them and even directed cannon fire; after all he had been trained as an artillery officer, and it was still his first love. There were skirmishes between French and British cavalry, particularly at the village of Genappe, where there was a narrow bridge. But as far as Napoleon was concerned, Ney had lost the British.

*

The Allied army began to filter into its positions around Mont St Jean in the early afternoon of the 17th. Staff officers were waiting with their dispositions, written by De Lancey to Wellington's precise specifications.

Wellington had placed the bulk of his light cavalry on the left flank, to the east, with the Hanoverian Landwehr and green-coated Nassauers, supported by Picton's Division of British and Bijlandt's Dutch Belgians. They were lined out on the road behind a hedge which ran along the ridge. To a gravel pit on their flank he directed the 95th Rifles and in the farmhouse just short of the crossroads, which would be his command position, placed the reliable light battalions of the King's German Legion under Baron Ompteda.

The heavy cavalry he kept at the rear of the crossroads with the Dutch light and heavy cavalry, and on his right flank, intermingled Hanoverian, British German, Brunswick and Nassau troops. To the large Chateau complex on the far right of the line, with its vital function of holding the flank, he sent Cooke's Guards Division of four battalions, and some Hanoverian and Nassau light troops.

The most important aspect of these dispositions was the fact that Wellington formed up mostly on the reverse slope of the ridge. The bulk of his army could not be seen by the French.

He still believed that Napoleon's main thrust would be to the west, and kept the majority of his force there with an entire Dutch division in Braine L'Alleud, which did not arrive in the field until late in the day.

The troops took their places in incessant rain which had lasted all day and would go on into the night. As Private

Matthew Clay of the 3rd Guards said: 'We marched on until we reached the summit of a hill in a clover field. We halted and there took off our knapsacks. The storm was still continuing with dreadful violence.'

Napoleon had followed his army up the road towards Brussels, and the last of his troops did not make it to what would become the battlefield until the morning.

It is worth noting that an army corps on the march takes up 250 yards for every thousand infantry, and three times that for the same number of cavalry. Six guns take up 600 yards. So a corps of 20,000 men will stretch for about eight miles. It is eight miles, incidentally, from Quatre Bras to Napoleon's command position on the battlefield of Waterloo, La Belle Alliance.

Napoleon settled into the farmhouse of Le Caillou at nightfall with his staff. In fact, like all his command headquarters, it had been designated as the 'Imperial Palace' some hours before.

*

Wellington rode from his ridge north along the road to Brussels and settled down for the night in an inn in the village of Waterloo. Outside the rain battered against the glass of the windowpanes. It would be a hard, wet night, but tomorrow would be the ultimate test of his ability as a general.

10

18 June, 5 am
Mont St Jean

Cornet Lemuel Shuldham had tried to sleep, but it was useless. They had been placed in bivouac some three hundred yards from the front of a farmhouse which lay between the lines and the village of Waterloo. The firing of cannon – he could not say whether it was their own or that of the enemy – continued until dark, and as the main part of the army and that of the French were on the other side of the hill, he and his comrades saw nothing of what passed, and merely heard the cannonade. Such was the heightened state of his feelings, however, that he could not help but imagine the effect of the shot and the blasts.

It continued to rain and thunder during the whole of the hours of darkness. The rain was like nothing he had seen or felt before. Hungry and cold, and wet through to the skin, he passed the most wretched night.

Shuldham was well aware that the Peer had chosen their position himself, and he was sure that, strategically, it made perfect sense. But he could not help but wish that the great Duke had taken more trouble to explore the place, for the ground upon which they had been forced to make their beds was a field of fallow upon which it had been nigh impossible to lie. But they had used their ingenuity. He and Mills had visited the big farmhouse and found it empty. In an adjoining small barn they had discovered an abundance of straw, quite enough to line the area of mud that was to pass as their beds for the night. They had also managed to bring back some wood, sending two troopers up for more, and from this they contrived to make a passable campfire.

And so, as the rain stilled the embers, they slept fitfully, lying beneath the heads of their horses, which had been tied together in a long line.

Every so often, as Shuldham tried and failed to count the minutes and the hours, one or other of the horses would take fright suddenly at a clap of thunder, and more than once he had felt a hoof come horribly close to his head. But as the dawn broke and he looked about, he was pleased to see that no one had been hurt.

In the pale light he could see now that the rye stood shoulder high, but it still bore the greenness that told the countryman's eye it was not quite yet ready for the harvest. Shuldham rubbed his eyes and shivered in the dawn.

Beside him, to both left and right, along the length of what appeared to be an unremarkable ridge, 15 miles to the south of Brussels, other men were stirring from sleep. Most were older than he, some younger, but all, like him, were standing up in clothes sodden with the rain of as wet a night as most of them had ever known, and all were looking about for familiar faces.

Around Shuldham an army was waking up. Close on 70,000 men, swearing and spitting and cussing and rubbing their aching limbs as they rose from the cold, hard ground on which they had passed the night. A night which, for one in every five of them, would be their last on earth.

All of them knew that, although they could not see them through the drizzling rain, across the valley below their elevated position, another army, stronger even than their own, was now engaged in the self-same activities.

Over there lay the French – men of their own ages. Men identical to them in many ways: farmers, labourers, artisans and men of trade, along with lawyers, doctors, writers and artists. Men of all sorts, who in other times might have been their friends. But men who now, on this morning of all mornings, as the sun began to rise over Belgium, were most certainly their enemies.

Soon, when that sun was high enough in the sky and when the mud had dried out sufficiently for the cannon-balls to bounce into their ranks, carrying away file after file in a welter of death, all of those men knew that they must meet in battle. For that was their purpose today. Napoleon, the great thief of Europe, had escaped from captivity and threatened once again to take Europe. And so it was up to this army, Shuldham's army, to defeat him.

Brushing off his scarlet tunic, Shuldham looked in a momentary panic for his head-dress and sword, and to his relief, found his soldier-servant, Knight, holding them. Some yards off, in a line, pegged together with the other officers' horses, he saw his mount, a splendid pale grey. They were, it was commonly averred, the finest, most resplendent unit of cavalry of the British army.

But this morning they did not all look so fine. In fact they looked as miserable a set of creatures as ever you saw, covered in mud from head to foot, the other ranks' white belts dyed with the red colour run from their coats. As if, he thought, they had already completed the bloody work they were soon to begin. He took comfort in the knowledge, imparted to him by Trotter, that Sir William Ponsonby, the general who commanded their brigade, had also commanded the brigade in the Peninsula with Wellington (although of course the Greys had not been a part of it there). Ponsonby had spotted him and had specifically asked, on account of his own ADC, Lieutenant Christie of the 5th Dragoons, being detained at Brussels, for him, Lemuel Shuldham, to accompany him as an extra aide-de-camp the previous day, the 17th, and on this day also.

Shuldham, the most recently commissioned officer in the regiment, was eager for this battle, keen to test his sword and with it his spirit. For with the exhilaration came fear. Fear of the unknown. The greater part of the men in the Greys, as fine as they looked on parade, had never been in battle before.

But a position on the staff was all that the young cornet might have wished for. Hadn't he heard that a man attached to the staff would see a great deal more of the battle and suffer much less than if he were in the ranks? All he might do in the latter case, surely, was to stand still and be shot. Whereas when he was part of the staff he would have to be constantly on the alert, carrying orders hither and thither and observing and hearing all that might be going on. Realising, to his horror, that he should probably be with the General now, he mounted and, with no more than a word to Knight, rode towards Brigade headquarters, which had been located the previous evening a short distance to the rear of the regiment.

Shuldham trotted in and was greeted by the General

and his aides with a bonhomie that made him feel instantly welcome. He had come home.

✳

Back in the Greys' lines, John Bishop stretched and blew on his cold, damp fingers. The rain was still falling. How, he wondered, could be possible for the heavens to hold this much water? Mid-June and still the morning was as cold as ever, thanks to the rain. Slithering in the mud which now covered the slope on which they had made their camp the previous night, Bishop found his horse and made sure that her nosebag was securely fastened. She had been tired out by the previous two days' march, first advancing to the sound of the guns and then retreating away from the French back here. To this stark, undulating crossroads, south of Brussels. He guessed that he might at least have cause to be thankful for something. For he doubted very much if they would move from here now. Nosey would not want to move. By Bishop's reckoning the Duke would want to fight a defensive battle and cling to the ridge along which he had placed his army. He would let the French come to him, and with this weather, that would mean advancing over ground that had been soaked by 17 hours of this rain. Bishop smiled. Poor bloody infantry. They would be up to their knees in it coming over the fields. It would be no easy thing for the horses either, but nothing like the thousands of poor buggers destined to make their way over the fields and up the hill towards the Allied lines.

All along the line the men were standing to. Some were seeing to their horses as others still tried to find some breakfast of their own, whatever they could. But now thoughts were turning to the matter in hand. From the rear of their lines he could hear the swish and turn of the armourer's grindstone, grinding the regiment's sabres to a razor edge. He drew his own and wiped the blade clean of the rain. It was fine, not a spot of rust. But, on inspection two days ago, Captain Poole had told him to get it sharpened.

He turned and, leaving his mount tethered, walked towards the armourer. Unsurprisingly, this morning there was a queue of men waiting for his services. Troop Sergeant Major James Russell stood in front of him and turned to greet him, both men agreeing that it was as filthy a morning as either had known.

Bishop, though, pointed to a small patch of blue in the steely grey sky. The sun was coming through. It would clear soon enough.

And he was right, for as he reached the armourer sergeant, the rain stopped, and with it the clouds parted to allow a ray of sunshine through.

The regimental armourer was a giant of a man named James Bray, from Captain Barnard's troop, two years in the regiment and formerly a blacksmith by trade. He took Bishop's blade, and with a precision born of custom, held it against the big granite stone which he worked with his foot on a pedal.

The blade sang and sparks flew from it as Bishop watched the edge turn blue keen. The swords were the 1796 model, the same that the Heavies had used in the Peninsula. They had been modelled on a 1775-issue Austrian sword with what was called a hatchet blade, curved to a point only on one side. A week ago, however, all the British heavy cavalry had been ordered to grind their weapons down at the tip so that the sword presented a 'spear' point, which would be just as effective at stabbing as it was at cutting. Some though, including himself, had not done so, but had accentuated the blade, trimming the hatchet into a longer curve. The effect, thought Bishop, would be like flaying a slice of bacon from a side of ham.

The big man handed the sword back, and being careful not to touch the blade, Bishop slid it into the metal scabbard. It would be blunt before the day was out. The thought pleased him, and walking back up the slope to find his horse, Bishop was equally pleased to feel the sun warm on his back drying his sodden clothes.

✳

Corporal John Dickson of Captain Vernor's F Troop had been awakened about five o'clock by his comrade John McGee, who had sprung up, shouting, 'Damn your eyes, boys, there's the bugle!'

Dickson had told him to shut up. 'You're hearing things, man. It's the horses' chains clanking, Jock.' But McGee was having none of it, 'Clankin' chains? What's that, then?'

Dickson had sat up, listened again to the noise, and in it caught the clear shrill note of a reveille call.

'Damn you, Jock, you're right.'

The troop were on their feet in a few minutes and set about finding breakfast. 'Stirabout' again, a gloopy mix of oatmeal and anything else you could find boiled up in water. Filthy stuff, thought Dickson, but better than nothing.

He was just finishing his portion when Sergeant Ewart

found him and drew him out on picket duty. Ewart, twenty years his senior, pointed to the slope and the enemy beyond. 'Over there, lad, and report what you see when you've done.'

Dickson nodded and, finding his horse, mounted and walked her up the slope, some 200 yards to their front. On cresting the hill, he found himself on a road and reined in. It was daylight now, and the sun was every now and again sending bright flashes of light through the broken clouds. But across the valley a low mist lingered, obscuring the enemy.

Directly below him, a regiment of green-coated King's German Legion riflemen was marching through the ripening green corn to the support of their comrades, who had occupied a walled farmhouse to the right of the high road and just in advance of the lines.

There was a beat of drum and then, past Dickson, marching with a swinging, confident step, came a regiment of Dutch infantry, followed by another, and then one of Belgians and two more. They turned off at the crossroads between high banks on to the plateau and to his left began to deploy on the slope. There must have been at least 3,000 of them, he thought, colours waving high and looking fine, in their blue coats with orange-and-red facings.

Gazing at the Netherlanders, Dickson noticed close behind them a party of the 92nd, Gordon Highlanders under the command of a man he recognised, a Captain Ferrier, from Belsyde, in Linlithgow. Urging his horse forward he rode to join them. He wished them all a good morning and enquired as to their state.

One of their corporals answered. They were Picton's men, brigaded with the 42nd, the Royals and the Cameron Highlanders in the old Fighting Division from the Peninsula.

All Scots together, thought Dickson. That was good. He wondered if they had suffered as badly as the Black Watch on the 16th.

The Corporal shook his head. Bad wasn't the word for it, he told him. There hadn't been a regiment that was there in Picton's command that hadn't lost a third of its men.

Dickson thought he must be exaggerating, but shook his head in sympathy.

The man went on. They had done worse than the Black Watch. Had lost half their men, killed, wounded and missing. And they had no more than ten officers left to them now. They had begun the day with thirty-six.

Dickson shook his head again and, taking his leave, returned to his post, where, pondering the Gordons' losses, he was taken by surprise by a battery of artillery, limbered up with six horses a piece, that came dashing along the road, directly in front of him, splashing his overalls with mud. Dickson cursed them, but supposed they would not understand his words. They looked like Hanoverians. They were not British certainly. He wondered if they might have been Dutch, or some other sort of German. God alone knew how many nations there were in this army of theirs.

As he watched, the battery, all four guns, drew up about a hundred yards in front of him and swung round off their limbers, barrels pointing into the valley.

And what he saw when he looked beyond the guns made him gasp. For the mist had cleared now and the valley was bathed in sunshine. From Dickson's vantage point, behind the low beech-trees that skirted the high banks of the sunken road, he could see the French army drawn up, directly opposite. Tens of thousands of them. They were, he reckoned, barely a mile from where he stood. There were great columns of infantry, and squadron after squadron of cavalry: Cuirassiers, red Dragoons, Hussars, and green Lancers with little red and white, swallow-tail flags at the end of their lances.

Most impressive of all, though, was a regiment of Cuirassiers that went dashing at full gallop over the brow of the opposite hill, with the sun shining on their steel breastplates.

It must have been around eight o'clock, he thought, when the general hubbub that filled the valley was broken by a sudden roll of drums along the whole of the enemy's line, and a few moments later music came from the bands of a hundred battalions. Dickson thought that he could recognise the tunes and then was not so sure, for such was the cacophony that the sounds became mixed and lost in uproar. And then it seemed to him that every regiment, every battalion on the opposite slope had begun to move. The French were taking position for battle. And at that moment he noticed that, while from the enemy lines came a din whose equal he had never heard, the Allied line seemed to have fallen perfectly silent.

11

Situation Report
18 June, Breakfast
Mont St Jean

The morning was wet and miserable. Most men had not found shelter and few had managed to find any food. The Emperor, of course, was different.

Breakfasting on chicken at Le Caillou, Napoleon told his staff: 'Wellington's a bad general and the English are bad troops. It will be a picnic.'

But as much as there was on the table before him and his marshals, Napoleon did not eat. He had no appetite. Perhaps because he knew he was lying.

*

On the Allied side of the valley, the ebullient Captain Cavalie Mercer of the Royal Horse Artillery and his men ate 'stirabout' and dug for potatoes in the kitchen garden behind La Haye Sainte. In the shelter of the wall of a hovel just behind the crossroads in the centre of the ridge, Rifleman Kincaid of the 95th boiled a camp kettle filled with tea, milk and sugar and served it up to the staff officers who passed by. Meanwhile Lieutenant James Hope of the Gordon Highlanders cut a steak from the hindquarters of a dead bullock, fastened it to a ramrod and held it over a fire.

*

Others, like Ensign Gronow of the 1st Foot Guards, were even luckier.

Gronow was a Welsh-born Old Etonian who had been commissioned into the First Guards (the Grenadier Guards) in 1812. At Eton he had been a great friend of the poet Shelley and knew many of the leading figures of his time, including Beau Brummel and Byron. At Waterloo he was just 21.

Gronow had just returned to his battalion, the 2nd Battalion 1st Guards, after having been made an aide-de-camp to General Picton, commander of the 5th Infantry Division, and was greeted by his friends, in particular Ensign Sam Burgess and Colonel William Stuart, the second-in-command of the battalion.

'How are you, old chap', said Stuart. 'What the deuce brought you here? Take a glass of wine and a bit of ham. It will perhaps be your last breakfast.'

Burgess called out: 'Come here, Gronow, and and tell us some London news.'

Burgess, according to Gronow, had made himself a sort of gypsy tent, with the aid of some blankets, a sergeant's halberd and a couple of muskets. 'My dear old friend was sitting on a knapsack, with Colonel Stuart, eating cold pie and drinking champagne which his servant had just brought from Brussels.' Apart from exceptions like this the Allied army was on subsistence rations and the usual tot of rum.

Horses were watered, and as dawn rose at 4 am, muskets were fired in the air to clear the barrels. The fields of standing crops were turned to mud and everything was soaked through.

✳

At breakfast Napoleon was informed that it would take until 11 am to drag the heavy artillery into place through the quagmire. His army was standing on the slope of another ridge facing that on which Wellington had drawn up his men. Napoleon had 54,400 infantry, 15,600 cavalry, 2,000 support staff and 246 guns.

Facing him were 71,150 Allied troops, including 53,800 infantry, 13,350 cavalry, 1,500 support staff and 134 guns. Of the infantry, just 13,000 were British and 6,000 of them had never fired a shot in anger. That was soon to change.

12

18 June, 11 am
Mont St Jean

Cornet Lemuel Shuldham found General Ponsonby with Major Reignolds and his extra aide-de-camp, Captain De Lacy Evans, riding to inspect the brigade, which was drawn up at the foot of a hill. This done, they made for the summit, where to his surprise, they found two gentlemen in plain clothes mounted on a pair of fine-looking horses. They were deep in conversation and surrounded by officers, looking as if they might as well be at a hunt meet.

All were looking towards the east; some of them, including the civilians, through glasses. As they approached the group, Evans turned to Shuldham and informed him quietly that the man in the round hat, the old man, was the Duke of Richmond. The other one, with the eye patch, was his son, Lord William Lennox.

Ponsonby greeted them with a polite 'Good morning' and enquired as to the son's health after his fall, during what he had heard had been a hard race.

Shuldham, like most officers in the army, knew well that Lennox had fallen heavily during a steeplechase that April, after which he had lain in a coma for three days and nights, not being expected to survive. By a miracle he had done so, now minus the sight of one eye, but of course he had been put on the sick list and would now miss the battle with his regiment. Clearly, though, thought Shuldham, he was determined to see what he could of it. Surely, he thought, this was the best place to be on the field, among such men, although at the same time he could not help but feel a sense of guilt at not being with the men of his troop and Captain Felton.

The elderly man lowered his glass and asked Ponsonby where he thought they might see the Prussians. Did he suppose they would come across? Ponsonby told him that Marshal Blücher had given his word, but if they did not they might find themselves hard-pressed.

Ponsonby, and with him Shuldham, Evans and Reignolds, joined the others in looking to the east, but they could see no-one.

Then one of the officers exclaimed: 'There, look, Sir. What's that? It's a Prussian hussar, is it not? A picket.'

Together, they strained to see. Shuldham, who had no field-glass, squinted and thought for a moment he could make out a shako and a black plume.

Richmond averred that it did look like a Prussian gentleman. But Ponsonby was still staring, adjusting his field-glass. At length he declared that the man was no Prussian after all but a French hussar with a green coat and pelisse. Shuldham had to agree with the General. There was no proof that the Prussians would come, and he wondered at how easily people's hopes could conjure things up into a desired shape.

✳

A hundred and fifty yards away down the slope, to Shuldham's left, Lieutenant Archibald Hamilton had also spotted a figure in the landscape. But this time there could be no mistaking its identity, nor did its appearance raise his hopes.

The figure rode a white horse, purer in colour than any of the Greys' own mounts and wore a simple drab grey topcoat. It was the head-dress, though, that gave him away, for it was the hat which had become familiar throughout the world these last thirty years. Surrounded by what could only be described as a cloud of staff, Napoleon was riding the length of his line, inspecting his troops.

Hamilton shouted to Captain Payne, pointing towards 'the great thief of Europe'.

*

The French were cheering now, all along the line, at the sight of the man who had taken them away from their farms and their families to fight in his name again, and restore at least some of the glory to France that she had lost on his abdication just over a year before. A common thought ran through the minds of the observers on the hill as they watched the man on the white horse. For all of them knew that this must be his last roll of the die, and that he, surely, thought he was going to make it count.

No one in the party of officers said a word, but they must all, thought Hamilton, be feeling as he did: simply disheartened and, not the least, afraid. One of the aides rode up to Uxbridge, who, Hamilton noticed, had ridden close to them and was speaking to the Duke of Richmond. The aide suggested he might rally the men and have them give three cheers for the Duke of Wellington.

Uxbridge stared at him for a few moments and then shook his head, replying that he doubted very much whether his Grace would want to cut cards with the devil.

The aide nodded and retired, somewhat deflated, but Shuldham, overhearing the exchange, guessed that Uxbridge was right. It was not the Duke's way. He had built his reputation in Spain on caution, and if they were to be victors that day, that was surely how the battle would be won. He wondered too whether the men had the stomach yet to cheer. He looked at the battalions grouped in the brigade around them and noticed that they had become very silent.

These were Picton's men and had suffered hard at Quatre Bras on the 16th. The two Highland regiments had been badly cut up and the Belgian infantry to their front now had lost almost one in three killed. He was sure, though, that when the time came the redcoats would hold. Certainly the Highlanders.

Hamilton had spotted Shuldham with the staff, and taking his leave for a moment, rode across. 'Lemuel, you lucky devil. With the staff! What news? Are we to fight today? We might yet again retreat on Brussels as we did yesterday.'

Shuldham replied that they would fight. Wellington knew this country and had selected the ridge. The talk was that he would nail himself to it, as he did at Bussaco. And Blücher had given his word that he would come.

They would have their battle.

✳

Ponsonby, seeing the two young officers in conversation, rode towards them. Looking at Hamilton, he asked whether he had received his letters asking him to join as an aide-de-camp.

Hamilton apologised. They had arrived only that morning.

Ponsonby said that he would enquire of Captain Payne himself, Hamilton's troop commander, and that he should now consider himself removed to his staff. Hadn't he promised his father that he would look out for him?

Ponsonby turned to De Lacy Evans, but just as he spoke, a gun opened fire. Ponsonby reached into his pocket and drew out the pocket watch that his own father had given him on purchasing his lieutenancy 25 years before. It had not lost a minute since.

He flipped it open. 'Thirty-one minutes past eleven. That, you might say, gentlemen, opens the battle.'

As more cannonballs began to fly along the line, it became evident that the entire French artillery must be opening up, although the effect of the cannonade was to produce such a cloud of white smoke that the French lines in all their grandeur were now barely visible.

Ponsonby turned to Hamilton. The newest aide should now 'make himself useful'. Take himself off on a gallop and visit each of the commanding officers of the brigade. He must tell them to withdraw their regiments back towards the base of the hill as close as possible. They didn't want to lose them before they had the chance to be at the enemy.

13

Situation Report
18 June, 12.30 pm

The battle probably opened at 11.30 am. When asked afterwards, no one seemed quite certain.

Napoleon had wanted to start his cannonade at 9 am but the ground was too soft to mount the guns quickly. When the Grand Battery did eventually open fire, the Allies immediately began to feel it. Cannonballs did not stop at the first impact. They hit the front rank of a unit and then hit the second rank and then they carried on, killing and maiming as they went. Two-thirds of Wellington's casualties, 12,000 men, were to be caused that day from artillery shot.

Standing over on the right wing, Ensign Leeke of the 1/52nd Foot remembered: 'The standing to be cannonaded and having nothing else to do is about the most unpleasant thing that can happen to soldiers in an engagement. I frequently tried to follow with my eye the course of the balls from our own guns which were firing over us . . . I distinctly saw the French artillerymen go through the whole process of sponging out one of the guns and reloading it; I could see that it was pointed at our square and when it was discharged I caught sight of the ball which appeared to be in direct line for me. I thought, shall I move? No, I gathered myself up and stood firm with the Colour in my right hand.'

Lieutenant Hugh Wray of the 40th Foot wrote: 'One shot killed and wounded 25 of the 4th Company; another of the same kind killed poor Fisher, my captain, and 18 of our Company; another killed or wounded 23. At the same time poor Fisher was hit I was speaking to him, and I got all his brains over me as his head was blown to atoms.'

*

The initial French attack came on Wellington's right wing, in an offensive against the chateau of Hougoumont. The chateau was manned by the Foot Guards: the two light companies of the Coldstream and 3rd or Scots Guards, 200 men under the command of a Scot, James Macdonnell. In the woods around the chateau were Nassauers and a Hanoverian Jager company. In all there were around 1,200 men.

At 11.30 the French attacked. Taking most of the wood, they drove the Hanoverians back. On the east of the chateau the 1st Guards under Lord Saltoun retook the orchard at 12.30, and the Coldstream and Scots Guards came round the west side and attacked into the woods.

More French were drawn in at 12.30 and attacked the west of the buildings, forcing the Guards back inside. At 1 pm a certain Lieutenant Legros, a giant of a man, and thirty others forced the North Gate and got inside, but they were shot to pieces, except for a drummer boy. Macdonnell, Lieutenant Henry Wyndham and the two Graham brothers closed the gates by force, along with two men from the Scots Guards and other officers. Wellington would later say that this one action had saved the battle. But just as the North Gate of Hougoumont was shut, over on the Duke's left flank, another crisis, just as dangerous, was about to unfold.

14

18 June, 12.30 pm
East of the Crossroads, Mont St Jean

Standing among the regimental lines, and still dismounted, much to his annoyance, John Bishop watched Lieutenant Hamilton ride off and then, looking to his right, gazed at the roundshot coming in from the French artillery. They appeared as tiny specks of black that flew across the valley, spangled now as it was by the morning sunshine. They looked harmless, but Bishop knew that they were deadly enough.

Sergeant Major Robertson walked over and called out his name. What new trouble was coming now, wondered Bishop, but the Sergeant Major was wearing a smile. Happy with the gin that Bishop had found for him.

As they turned to watch the enemy, it occurred to Bishop that the French guns were lessening their fire now on the Allied right. Either that or else the guns on the French right, opposite their own position, which had not fired yet, were now opening up. Either way it was becoming clear that very soon they would be the target.

Robertson spoke to the group of troopers to their front and was told that the French were sighting their guns. They should keep their heads down.

Lieutenant Wyndham rode up with orders from Brigade. They were ordered into line. Wyndham barked the order, 'The regiment will mount. We are to retire beyond that hill.'

He pointed, and looking to their rear, Bishop saw the crest of another small slope.

With little fuss, they mounted and rode to it in line, going down the other side. Before them lay a cobbled road, the highway from Charleroi to Brussels, and alongside it, some four hundred yards away, was a farm surrounded by high whitewashed walls.

Bishop turned to Robertson and asked the Sergeant Major what the farm might be.

That, he was told, was 'Mount Saint Jean' and from now on it was a field hospital. He prayed that he would not end up in there. Not in a field hospital. Better off dead than under the surgeon's saw. A cannonball would kill you, or might take off an arm or a leg. But Bishop also knew the damage a musket ball could do. Small enough, but one shot through an arm or a leg and that was enough to lose the limb. Better to die from a sabre cut. Though the French didn't cut, they thrust. So better to die from a thrust to the heart then. He pushed the thoughts from his mind, and as they settled their mounts, listened as the French bombardment grew in volume.

From time to time a cry signified that the roundshot had found their target. And then, as he watched, cannonballs began to bounce on the crest of the slope and towards them. The first to hit their group bounced three times, even on the sodden ground, and then seemed to lose its momentum; but nevertheless, rolled into the leg of one of the forward troopers' mounts, and to Bishop's astonishment, took it clean away. The horse screamed and collapsed on its bloody stump, flinging off the hapless trooper. Bishop gazed in horror. He had thought the force of the round had been spent.

The Sergeant Major gave him a word of warning. He might think that, but those balls still carried a lot of weight. He had seen many a man stick out his foot to stop one, only to lose it.

*

More roundshot was coming at them now. One of the troopers was hit and knocked from the saddle, his left side a gaping, bloody hole. He screamed as he fell.

Bishop heard Colonel Hamilton call out above the noise, 'Greys! They have found us again.'

Wyndham raised his voice in command. 'Form open column. Half squadrons. The regiment will retire fifty paces.'

This time the French did not take so long to find them, and this time with the roundshot came shell, exploding over their heads and showering down lethal shards of red-hot metal. The horses whinnied and Bishop patted his own on the neck.

A shell burst some yards in front of him, high but close enough to Major Hankin, who was out in front, with the Colonel, in command of the right-hand number 1 squadron of the three that made up the regiment. Fragments of the case fell around, but none hit Hankin. However, as Bishop watched, he saw the Major's horse rear and shy, and then the officer was off. Hankin landed well, rolled away and narrowly missed being trampled, but it was clear as he tried to stand that he was hurt. He wobbled and lost his balance. A trooper jumped down and rushed over to help him as he fell. The battle was over for Major Hankin before it had properly begun.

Colonel Hamilton, who himself had narrowly avoided being hit, turned his horse to where Hankin stood, supported on the trooper. Having taken a careful look at his second-in-command he found Major Poole, who had command of the centre squadron.

'Major Poole, Major Hankin is obliged to quit the field. Your post is now to command the right squadron.'

Poole nodded his head: 'Colonel, if you please, I wish to remain with my troop.'

Hamilton smiled, 'As you wish. It is your prerogative.' He turned and rode to Brevet Major Cheney and from what Bishop could see, ordered Cheney to take command of the squadron.

Bishop was about to comment on this to the Sergeant Major when the ground before them, beyond the hedge some fifty yards distant, suddenly filled with men. They wore blue uniforms and for an instant Bishop was startled, thinking they must be French. But then he saw the shakos in the style of their own infantry, and the orange and white facing colours, and realised they were Belgians. And they were in full flight.

The air filled with shouts which Bishop thought were from the Belgians, but then recognised English words. The British troops either side of the retreating Belgian infantry were jeering them.

The man to Bishop's right, a recent young recruit from Ambleside named Tom Dawson, who had once been a labourer, pointed at them and snarled that they were cowards. He implored Bishop to look at them, and to curse them for not standing to fight.

Bishop pushed down his pointing hand and told Dawson the men weren't cowards, that they'd just had enough. Bishop looked at them. They were all in. They had been beat up at Quatre Bras and they weren't going to take it again.

The Highlanders were still jeering, but Bishop thought that at least was fair enough, for he knew well how badly they too had been mauled at the crossroads. Yet they were standing. They would face the French.

Whatever their allegiance, the Belgians of Bylandt's brigade had bolted almost without firing a shot, and left the Highlanders and the rest of Picton's 'Fighting 5th' division to meet the whole French attack on the British left centre.

*

From their position a little distance to the rear of the hedge, Bishop could hear now the crack of musketry as the redcoats tried to stem the tide of the French advance. White smoke, gunsmoke, began to drift towards them up the hill from beyond the road.

Colonel Hamilton was directly in front of them now, chatting to one of his aides, Lieutenant Carruthers, Bishop thought it was, as if he was making small-talk at a ball. He turned away from their conversation, however, as Sir William Ponsonby came riding up, trotting fast on his little bay hack, followed by his aide-de-camp, De Lacy Evans.

Bishop watched as the two men met and Ponsonby pointed to the valley. The Colonel spoke to Wyndham and then the adjutant was bellowing, 'The regiment will advance to the beech hedge.'

They moved as one up to the hedge and then Ponsonby and Hamilton crossed over it, landing their horses in the road beyond. Bishop followed their line of sight and there, beyond the three regiments of Highlanders, the Royal Scots and the 4th, all clearly visible despite the smoke, their colours billowing in the hurricane of battle, he saw the French. Thousands of them. They were coming on up the hill in three columns, drums beating and colours flying, beneath the gilded eagles. And all that stood between them and Brussels now, thought Bishop, was what he could see around him. The Highlanders, the redcoats and with them, the Greys.

16

18 June, 1 pm
Mont Saint Jean

The roundshot came careening in high over the ridge. Sergeant Major William Crawford of Captain Barnard's troop watched them fly, and began to wonder if they would not all be blown to pieces before they saw any action. At least, he reflected, they were dismounted. Less of a target.

As he thought this, the order came to 'advance a little', so as to be more in cover of the crest of the rising ground to their front. They led their horses up, towards where their own guns were positioned, and in doing so found themselves indeed less exposed. They were standing, Crawford could see now, in a dip in the ground, a hollow, and were also far in advance of the other regiments of their brigade, the Inniskillings and Royals, who were still being punished by the enemy gunfire. As Crawford watched, one man of the Royals was decapitated in a welter of blood and brains that spattered the men around him. Crawford turned to Captain Barnard and proposed that they suggest to the Inniskillings that they also move forward.

Barnard stared at the balls flying in with apparent indifference and shook his head, answering that it was their commander's decision. Crawford nodded and turned away. It was always thus with officers, even good ones like Captain Barnard.

An orderly rode up to Barnard. Another order. 'Wheel right, half squadrons.'

Mounting now, they turned from line and formed easily, as if on a parade ground, into an open column.

No sooner had they done so, however, than the adjutant barked out again, 'Wheel left, into line.'

Just as they had done so many times at Canterbury, the regiment moved in the prescribed manner into two lines of three squadrons, A troop of each in front, B Troop fifty yards behind. Crawford wondered what the brigade commander was intending.

Close to where Crawford sat, Colonel Hamilton, positioned on the road, heard a halloo and saw a red-coated figure galloping towards them from the direction of the command position at the crossroads. The galloper saw Sir William Ponsonby, who was deep in conversation with Colonel Hamilton. It was clear, thought Hamilton that the General was the focus of his attention.

Ponsonby too had seen him coming and was ready. He smiled at the aide. The boy was breathless, but managed to deliver the orders that Wellington wished the heavy brigade to charge the enemy immediately. 'They could no longer be awaited.'

Ponsonby, amused by the wording of the order, raised an eyebrow: 'Very well.' He nodded to the aide. 'You may inform his Grace that his dragoons will do their utmost. You may go.' The boy rode away and Ponsonby continued: 'Colonel Hamilton, to your post if you please. All officers will take posts. Trumpeter, sound the advance.'

Hamilton turned his horse, and with a parting nod to Ponsonby, rode for the centre of the line, towards where Major Poole still sat doggedly with his own men.

Immediately behind the hedge line to the south of the road and closest to him stood a battalion of British infantry, drawn up in line three deep. He saw their colour fluttering in the wind, navy blue, and recognised it as that of the 1st of Foot, the Royal Scots. They had not yet engaged the enemy and were standing at the ready, awaiting their next command.

Hamilton found Poole and then turned to his own trumpeter, 'Buncle, sound the advance.'

'The regiment will advance to the attack.' A pause, then, 'Advance. Walk-march.'

The trumpet went up to Buncle's lips and the notes seemed to energise the regiment like an electric charge. As one, the men kicked in their legs and slowly the great grey horses began to move. Slowly, at the walk at first and then at a trot, the entire line of the Scots Greys, 444 officers and men, began to advance up the incline behind which they had been sheltering, towards the road.

From beyond they could hear a great noise now. To Crawford it sounded like hundreds of blacksmiths beating hammers on so many frying pans.

Hamilton drew his sabre and held it tight against his shoulder, his arm at right angles to his body. He turned to see the men, and then turning back to face the enemy, with a magnificent flourish raised his sword and waved it in the air three times.

'Hurrah. Hurrah, boys! With me. Death to the French!'

Again, almost as one, the squadron immediately behind

their Colonel gave voice, closely followed by those on its left and right. 'Death to the French!'

Hamilton rode at the hedge and leapt it with an easy bound. To his left and right men of the first squadron were doing the same, as if engaged in some great steeplechase.

Those to the rear landed hard, putting up red dust from the rough dirt road which ran the length of the ridge, and went through the crossroads before taking the second hedge. Aware now of red-uniformed infantry to his front, Hamilton pulled up and saw the others do the same until all the men were barely at a trot.

He felt alive as never before. Everything was working in concord, his body, his horse, his hand, clenched tight on the grip of his sabre. All seemed to have come together at this one moment. And he sensed that he was not alone in the sensation.

Surely, thought Hamilton, if the enemy can hear us now, when they see us, they will simply run before we have a chance to be at them. All through the ranks to his rear, the men followed their Colonel's example, waving their swords in the air until told curtly by their sergeants to replace them in the correct position for the advance.

To his surprise and alarm, he could now see, however, that many of the infantry to his front were not turned to the enemy but were facing to the rear and walking back towards him and the regiment. Could the British infantry be in retreat? Had their order come too late to save the day?

Sergeant Major Crawford too had found the infantry. They came walking back towards him, wounded and bloody. They were in good order, but there was no doubt

about it, they were pulling back. For a moment Crawford instinctively slowed his horse, but then he continued,
keeping in line with the others.

There were Highlanders among the redcoats and
Crawford had to swerve a little to avoid them. Then,
hearing the officers shouting to the retreating infantry he
did so himself. 'Come on, turn, lads. We can beat them.
Look, we're here. Come on. Scotland forever!'

Hamilton was yelling it too now, and then more voices
from the Highlanders took up the cry. 'Scotland forever!'
More followed and the Greys themselves, shouting at the
tops of their voices.

Hamilton called out to the squadron commander,
'Hold. Hold your ground.' And still the infantry came on
towards them. But this was no rout. The men walking
towards him were not in a headlong rush. There was still
time, thought Hamilton. He knew that timing was crucial
now. Uxbridge's order had not been a second too soon.
Other redcoated infantry were coming now, through the
intervals in the squadrons of the Greys. He had to stop
them.

He called out to a group of a dozen kilted Highlanders,
men of the Gordons, who had turned and were moving
back towards the rear, towards him.

'Turn back, my brave lads. Face the front. We're with
you now. Scotsmen together. Look, boys. We're the Greys.
The Greys are with you, men. We'll push them back.
Death to the French.'

The Highlanders saw him and stopped, and in an
instant he saw their faces seem to hearten and then the
men were turning and rallying to their front, calling to

their comrades, to the left and right. One of their officers, a young lieutenant who had been following his men, attempting to rally them, looked up at Hamilton.

'Thank God.'

Around him Hamilton could see that his officers and men were now exhorting the infantry to return, and in most cases with success. He urged his horse forward until he was in the thick of them, surrounded by the kilted infantry.

*

John Dickson too was in their midst with Vernor's troop. He saw their Brigadier, Sir Denis Pack, turn to the Gordons, and to his surprise heard him shout quite clearly. 'Ninety-second, you must advance! All in front have given way.'

The Highlanders began to press forward to a ragged line of bushes that grew along the face of the slope in front, shouting as they ran. Then, twenty yards out from the French, they stopped. Commands were shouted and Dickson saw them present and fire. The French line dropped.

Ponsonby was beside them now, along with De Lacy Evans, almost with Dickson himself for a moment. But passing him they moved to the front of the line, and at that moment De Lacy Evans waved his hat.

And then Dickson heard the Colonel's voice. 'Now, Scots Greys. Now. Charge!'

As he watched he saw Colonel Hamilton wave his sword in the air and a great cheer rose from the ranks. Dickson dug his spurs into Rattler, and the horse carried him fast towards the French.

All along the ridge the great grey line of horses were moving forward now, heads down, manes flowing, hooves tearing at the muddy turf.

The noise was like a thunderstorm, and yet above it Dickson heard the sound of the Highland pipers. He tried to make out the tunes and thought one might be Johnny Cope. But it was lost as quickly as it came, and then the Greys began to descend the slope, into the inferno below.

❋

Together with the redcoated infantry they moved. Crawford glanced quickly to his left and right to see the regiment still in line, and then, looking to his front, he gasped.

He could see the French plain as day now. A great blue-black mass of them. Thousands of men, their muskets at the high porte, bayonets gleaming in the sun, with their officers high on horses, their shakos topped with waving white plumes, and there, bobbing in the midst of the mass, the golden eagle-topped standards, trailing their tricolours. The French were marching out of the corn, up the slope, straight towards them. And they were now just some 60 yards away.

There was a sudden shouted command from Captain Barnard, and another from the Colonel, but amid the growling din of the endless cannon fire and musket-balls whizzing past his ears, Crawford could hear neither of them. He knew, though, what it must be and drew his sabre from its scabbard on his left side. The shimmering, wickedly sharp blade came free with a hiss, and Crawford settled the pommel of the hilt on his right hip. There was a thud from his immediate right and front, where Lieutenant James Gape, the youngest lieutenant in the regiment had come across, and Crawford saw that a musket-ball had hit Gape's saddle. The boy looked appalled. Crawford smiled and shouted above the din, 'Better there than in you, Sir.'

*

They were walking on again now, the lines re-dressed just as they should be, the trumpets calling their siren notes, and slowly they broke into another, gentle trot, starting to descend the slope into the valley. A little way down the hill, the redcoated infantry stopped, and for a moment Crawford wondered aghast if they had lost their nerve and might be about to retreat again. He needn't have worried.

As he watched, the British line loaded their muskets, biting open the cartridges, spitting the charge down the barrel and ramming it home. Then they came swiftly up to the 'present', muskets levelled. In each of the two regiments, the Gordons and the 1st Foot, officers barked a command and then, with a crash and a cloud of dense white smoke, the British line spat flame and death at the French. Men were thrown back by the force of the volley. The blue mass flinched and seemed to sway.

*

Looking across to his right, Crawford could see the crossroads in plain view now, and there, beneath a tall elm tree, astride his horse, the unmistakable figure of Wellington in his blue frock coat. Directly to the Commander's front he saw the Household Brigade, led by Uxbridge himself, as its three regiments broke into a gallop and charged down the slope behind the farmhouse. And then he knew that now, at last, within minutes, seconds, it would be their turn.

On his immediate right and slightly in advance of their own squadron line, lay the Royals, and then suddenly there was Ponsonby with them, at their front, shouting a huzzah and flourishing his sword. And now, with no word of command, they were off, behind the General, hallooing their war cries as they went.

∗

Crawford watched as, shaken by the British volley, the French column came to a halt to their front. He muttered beneath his breath, 'Break, damn you. Break!'

But the French column did not break. Shaken as they were, they stood, and then he saw the front two ranks raise their muskets and aim for him and his comrades. There was a crackle of fire and flames came spouting from the muzzles. Musket-balls, two of them, shot past Crawford's right cheek and left leg. To his right, someone fell. He looked at him and wished he had not. Sandy Black, the weaver from Dunfermline, had been shot through the throat and was gouting dark blood, his eyes bulging, mouth open in a noiseless cry. Other men had been hit too, but some only slightly. And, what was more, none of the horses had turned. Now it was the French infantry's turn to waver. He wondered what they would do. Try to load and fire another ragged volley? Try to stop the redcoated cavalry? Or cut and run in the *sauve qui peut,* with every man for himself before the pounding, crushing hooves of the big grey horses.

Barnard was yelling with a new urgency now, and the other officers too, along the length of the line. To his left one of the younger privates, Isaac Bell, just turned 17, seemed to be shaking in the saddle. Crawford turned to him and told him to remain calm.

But Crawford too was shaking, although he was trying not to show it. He could see that the French were forming squares now, and knew that should they succeed in completing the complex manoeuvre, all would be lost, for there was no way that cavalry could penetrate the solid mass of bayonets of a good square. But then he saw that the nearest square was not yet complete, and indeed none of them had been closed.

Barnard had seen it too, and with a shout rallied his troop. 'Charge, charge the square. View halloo. Charge!'

Together the troop, oblivious as to what the rest of the squadron or the regiment might be doing, pushed directly at the French, just making it into a gallop, and were on them in seconds, before the ranks had time to close.

✳

With Barnard's men, at the unformed square, William Crawford raised his sword, felt its weight, saw it shine silver-blue in the watery sunlight and prayed for salvation. He watched in fascination as, guided by his hand, it swung down upon the head of the nearest Frenchman standing in front of him, whose bayonet-tipped musket was pointed at his chest. For an instant Crawford had an impression of the man's face, unshaven, with bad black teeth and bright green eyes. Then the blade hit the Frenchman's tall black shako and sliced through it as one might through a piece of ripe fruit. And it carried on slicing downwards through the man's head in the same way and Crawford was for a moment aware of the two halves of the head falling away from each other, the face bisected from the back of the head like a mask. But instantly his sword was falling again as he turned his attention to the next man in line. Looking to his left he was aware of Bell doing the same. The boy was grinning now, and Crawford knew that he would be fine, lost as he was in the heat and the fury and the joy of the killing.

17

Situation Report
18 June, 1.15 pm

At 1 pm the 80 guns of the French Grand Battery had opened up on the Allied left, and a few minutes later D'Erlon's corps attacked. Napoleon threw in all five divisions with 33 battalions, 16,000 infantry in all, supported by Cuirassiers on their left and Lancers and Chasseurs on their right.

They formed into assault divisions and began to attack at five-minute intervals, advancing across the valley and up the slope of the ridge. They moved through the mud and tall crops, taking about twenty minutes to get to the hedge line.

Most never made it. In front of them the already weakened Dutch Belgians of Bijlandt's brigade broke and retired. But the dense French formations suffered from the British guns, and when their lead columns crested the ridge they were decimated by fire from Picton's infantry, who had deployed from column into line.

The redcoats fired blind into the smoke and towards the the cries of '*Vive l'Empereur*'. At the same time a skirmisher shot Picton through the head.

It was at that moment that Wellington unleashed the Heavy Brigade.

18

18 June, 1.30 pm
The Valley

A little distance away from Crawford and Barnard's troop, Vernor's men had not yet made contact with the enemy. Francis Kinchant dug his spurs into the flanks of his horse and pushed forward. He looked to his left and saw, close behind him the ranks of his own troop followed by B Troop under Fenton. They were all there, Sergeant Major Macwilliam, Sergeant Tannock, Dickson and the others, Butler, Craig, Harkness, Liddle, the two Turners from Kelso and from Alnwick. All together. There was John Turner, the baker's boy, who had disgraced himself last night and was on a charge. Kinchant would have to deal with him later. He cursed himself for such a thought at a moment like this.

He looked to his right. There was his coverman, Corporal Dickson, and beyond him he could see John Mills, his friend, yelling for all he was worth and grinning as he went. Captain Vernor was there too, out in front with the trumpeter, Joe Reeves, at his side, his sword raised high, almost in amongst the French now.

There was another man up close to the Captain, Sergeant Ewart, riding out in front of the troop. Ewart, the man who, more than any other, had nurtured him during the difficult early days just after he had joined the regiment.

There was no need to use the spurs now. The slope was impelling them forward and the French were so dense before them they could hardly move. And then they were on them, in among the French so close that he could smell them. Could see the look in their eyes. Could feel their fear.

✳

Up level now with Kinchant, where the slope grew steeper, John Dickson tightened his grip on the reins. There, among the corn, he could make out the black feather bonnets of the Highlanders, and could hear their officers ordering them to wheel back, by sections. A moment more and he was among them, as F Troop smashed into the French column. Dickson cut and thrust about him, and was aware of Colonel Hamilton ahead of him, careering past the British guns and down the slope. Looking up he saw that the man before him was Sandy Armour from Mauchline, kinsman of Jean Armour, Rabbie Burns's wife. And there was Sergeant Ewart on the right, at the end of the line just beside Cornet Kinchant, as always.

Rattler, unable to discriminate between friend and foe, kicked one of the redcoats and Dickson had no way to apologise or make good as the man fell with a groan. It was too bad. Most, though, had time to jump clear as the Greys thundered through. The cry was still on the lips of the horsemen, 'Scotland forever!' and the Highlanders returned it again. Dickson's heart leapt with pride and he grasped his sabre still tighter.

He was aware of hands at his legs, and realised that some of the Highlanders were trying to grab hold of the stirrups to pull themselves into the melee.

The air was a cacophony of noise, Highlanders and Greys, shouting with blood-lust, Frenchmen screaming as they fell or ran in panic to get away from the great grey horses.

Dickson focused again and found himself looking at a Frenchman. A young officer of Fusiliers. The man saw him too, and as their eyes met he slashed at Dickson, but the horseman, towering above him, parried the blow with ease and in doing so twisted the man's arm, which snapped like a twig with the pressure. The Frenchman fell to the ground, screaming, to be trampled under Rattler's hooves as Dickson carried on.

There was a sudden sharp crack of musketry to his left, and Dickson saw that they had been seen by a second French column. The trumpeter, Reeves, who was riding alongside him, sounded the Rally, and within what seemed like moments redcoated dragoons were swarming up from all sides, Greys among them but also some Inniskillings and Royals. Although Dickson could see no officer, Ewart was with them and several sergeants from the other regiments, and under their direction the motley unit made for the French column.

Within five minutes they had cut our way through as many thousands of Frenchmen. Dickson was in the thick of them now. Armour was still up with him and Ewart out in front.

He was unable to see five yards in front of himself for the smoke. The stench of it filled his nostrils as the sounds around him filled his head. Everywhere the noise of men and horses, frantic shrieks and others begging for mercy; and dominant over it all, the screams of the dying.

*

Close to Dickson, Francis Kinchant brought up his sabre and, selecting one man in front of him, just as Sergeant Ewart had told him to do, brought it down upon him, slicing at the left shoulder.

He had not expected the cut to be so clean, so smooth, or the effect so terrible. As the man fell apart, Kinchant carried on, his sabre doing fresh work. Dickson was with him, looking out for the Cornet as was his job, and up ahead he could see Ewart, the giant of a man, raising his sword again and again, it seemed to him, even here with balletic grace. He saw Ewart heading for a French officer and pushed through the mass to follow him.

Ewart cut at the Frenchman, a dismounted infantry colonel with a white plume on his shako, from the left and the man parried. But the sergeant was too good for him as Kinchant had known he would be, and with a flurry worthy of the fencing salle he turned the man's blade and it fell to the ground.

Then, to Kinchant's horror, he saw that Ewart had raised his sword again and was about to cut the disarmed French officer through the head. The man was crying, pleading with Ewart. 'Non, non. Mercy, mercy, Angleterre!' Kinchant shouted: 'Sar'nt Ewart. Don't kill him. Spare him.'

With some difficulty and using all his strength, the Sergeant changed the direction of the blade in mid-swing and brought the sword down through the air. Kinchant heard the hiss. He looked for Corporal Dickson but the man was lost in the melee. Turning back, Kinchant was met by the terrified gaze of the Frenchman who was as white as a sheet.

He was next to Ewart now. 'Sar'nt, we must make him prisoner. Give him quarter, man. He has surrendered.'

Ewart shrugged and looked at Kinchant with wide eyes which told him that this was a battlefield, no place for quarter. It was a killing ground. Then he nodded. 'Very well, Mister Kinchant, Sir. Your prisoner he is.'

The Frenchman, meanwhile, had retrieved his sword from the mud and held it to Kinchant, pommel first. Kinchant dropped to speak to him and smiled. 'Merci, mon Colonel. Allez vous en arrière.'

He accepted the man's sword and indicated the way to the rear. Looking in that direction, he had expected to see his regiment. But there were no dragoons there now, only infantry, for all were up with him and Ewart, or had gone far beyond, further in to the screaming blue mass of dying Frenchmen. He looked back to the front and saw first the carnage and then the officer. For the man had not yet gone. Instead, to Kinchant's horror, he saw that the officer was holding a pistol and that it was pointed at him. He said something, or at least thought that he did. But there were no words.

And the Frenchman too thought that he might have heard a word, just before he squeezed the trigger and sent the stupid English boy to oblivion.

✳

Further forward just beyond Ewart, amid the carnage that had been d'Erlon's corps, Hutchinson, the trumpet bumping hard against his side, swung his sabre high over his head and brought it down on the shako of a French-man below, slicing through the black top and into the skull. He felt the impact as metal hit bone and the razor edge cut in. Beneath him the man folded up, blood spouting from the wound. Hutchinson rode on oblivious, and then he saw it. Waving above the ranks, the Eagle.

He had dreamed of this. To take an Eagle. He had read in dispatches of the one taken at Talavera and how the man who had captured it had been promoted. Perhaps that would happen to him now if he could only take the bird.

He spurred towards the Eagle but got too caught up in the mass of men. His horse, nostrils flared and white teeth bared, bit at them as he dug in his spurs to her flanks. His sabre rose again and came down, cutting a man in two from the shoulder to the waist. Hutchinson did not hear the screams. On he went. Deeper into the crowd, towards the golden bird on the pole. As he approached, he saw that the colour was protected by two men, each armed with a halberd. While he watched another trooper cut at the left-hand escort, and the man fell to the ground. Hutchinson rode straight at the right-hand man, who thrust the halberd at him. Hutchinson parried the weapon away and then, raising his sword, cut down through the man's shako and into his skull. He was on the Eagle-bearer now, a young officer armed with slim infantry sword. Hutchinson grinned and prepared to attack, but as he raised his sword-arm again, something jabbed at his side from the left. He turned and moving his arm down, tried to parry the bayonet from his ribs. But it was too late. In horror he felt the slim steel blade slide fast into his side. He gasped, then screamed, before he fell.

❇

The Cuirassiers had come at them from the left, and Ewart had seen them from several hundred yards away. But their charge had been impeded by the mass of their own infantry, and by the time they reached the Greys any impetus had been lost. Ewart cut at the first to reach him and his aim was good. The sword hit the man on the jaw and nothing his helmet or body armour could do could prevent the Scotsman's sword from taking his life. Another man met a similar fate and then the Cuirassiers seemed to melt away. It seemed to Ewart that there had been barely two squadrons of the armoured cavalry and, swamped by the infantry, unable to manoeuvre, they soon began to retire.

Ewart was moving forward again, when he heard the report of a pistol behind him. He knew what it was before he turned. Sure enough, there was Kinchant, falling backwards over his horse, the life gone from him.

Turning his horse now, pulling hard at the reins, he watched as the French officer tucked his pistol under his coat. Ewart felt the anger rise inside him, and fully round now, pushed back towards the Frenchman. The officer looked at him and again begged for his life. Ewart smiled and for a moment, thinking he had got away with killing Kinchant, the Frenchman smiled and raised his hands to the heavens. But then his expression changed to one of horror, as Ewart raised his sabre and spat the words at him, 'Ask God for mercy. You'll get none from me,' and with one stroke of his sabre, his full body-weight behind it, the Sergeant brought down the blade and severed the man's head from his body.

Without pausing, Ewart brought his horse round again and found himself suddenly, frighteningly, alone. All the regiment, it seemed, and indeed the brigade, had gone off in twos and threes chasing the Cuirassiers.

Then, perhaps four hundred yards distant, in an open space among some bushes, he made out a small body of French infantry. A half-dozen of them. They were formed in a line and firing at a body of British infantry who had come down the slope and into the melee. Careful not to attract attention, Ewart trotted towards them. He had gone only a few yards when a shot whizzed past his left side from behind. Looking round, he saw that it had come from a wounded French tirailleur who was lying on the ground.

The man was reloading now, keen to try another shot, and Ewart, turning his horse again, rode back and, leaning far from the saddle, cut him swiftly and simply through the head.

Recovering and turning back, he prepared to re-engage the enemy and then was on them, slashing right and left. And now Ewart realised with relief that he was no longer alone. On his left Corporal Dickson, poor Kinchant's coverman, and another trooper, James Armour, of Fenton's troop, had come up. Dickson shouted to Ewart. 'Mister Trotter's dead. Come on, Sergeant.'

It was all that he needed. Together, the three of them charged into the French. Ewart dispatched one of them with a quick cut to the head and another with a deft backstroke. Then, as he made for the officer with the Eagle, he was horribly aware of a bayonet thrust dangerously close to his thigh. But Dickson was there. Parrying the musket away, he riposted and skewered the Frenchman with the spear point of his sabre as Ewart advanced on the Eagle-bearer. Armour and Dickson had worked hard and the officer was all that was now left of the group.

In his gloved left hand he held the blue-painted flagpole of an Eagle, the tricolour flying in the furious, bullet-whipped wind of the battlefield, its end secured in the socket of a white cross belt. In his right hand he held a straight, thin sword. It was dark with blood, and beside him, lying in the mud, Ewart could see the bare-headed body of a Grey. It was Hutchinson, Captain Payne's trumpeter. The boy was dead, and in an instant Ewart knew what he must do. Watched by Dickson and Armour, he rode for the officer, sword held out, ready to make a cut. He pulled up a few feet away and then closed, and for a few minutes, and what seemed like an eternity, the two men played cat and mouse, each of them acting on the defensive.

Then, his patience exhausted, the officer thrust for Ewart's groin. It was well done, but the big man parried the short infantry sword with ease, shattering its slight straight blade with the sheer weight of his own. He cut down at the man, slicing nicely into his head. As the Frenchman fell, still clutching the precious Eagle, Ewart grabbed at it and, wresting it from the dying Frenchman's grasp, pulled it towards him with his left hand. He found it surprisingly heavy; the pole was long and it proved at once difficult to carry. He tried to hold it at the same time as using his sword-arm but found it impossible, then, thinking of the flag, wrapped the colour around his bridle-arm so that the pole dragged on the ground, but the Eagle itself rested on his arm. This, he thought, was the trick, and he began to ride through the mud to catch up with the rest of the regiment. And then he heard the sound of someone coming on behind him and the snorting of a horse. He cast a quick glance backward, just in time to see a green-coated Lancer closing in on him, the red and white pennon of his lance edging horribly close to his back. Green coat. Brass helmet. The same Lancers, he thought, who'd done for the Highlanders at Quatre Bras.

There was nothing for it but to turn. Ewart pulled on the reins and made his horse turn to the left so that the lance would not catch him. The Lancer rode past a short distance, just missing him, and himself turning raised his lance like a javelin and hurled it at Ewart.

It was not a good throw and the missile came quite slowly. Slow enough for Ewart to watch it and, though it grazed his side, he was able to parry it away to the right. The lancer meanwhile had drawn his sword, but in the time it took him to do so, Ewart moved fast towards him. His mind was calm, surprisingly calm, he thought. He wondered how he should tackle the man and settled on cut number 3 from the cavalry Sword Manual, which he could almost recite from cover to cover. The great sabre cut the air in front of Ewart almost at right angles to his body, across the direction of the horse. He drove it in a semi-circle up from the left and, just as he had intended, caught the Lancer with an uppercut that took him in the chin. The blade carried on through the teeth and into the mouth. The man tried to scream, but his throat had gone in a bloody froth.

The mangled Lancer toppled from his horse, but the struggle had caught the eye of a French infantry officer on foot, a tall man of, he thought, perhaps six foot two. The man was pointing to Ewart and shouting for help. Six French infantrymen moved towards him now, one of them firing. The shot missed, zinging past Ewart's head, and the next instant the big trooper was on the infantryman, who had moved in with the bayonet. He swept away the man's musket and again cut hard down and into his skull.

The officer was desperate now, screaming at the other Frenchmen to load and fire, but Ewart turned and, seeing a gap in the melee, pushed on and, squeezing with his thighs, urged his wild-eyed horse back towards the Allied lines.

19

18 June, 2 pm
The Valley

Lemuel Shuldham had passed straight through the French. He had lost count of the number of them he had killed and maimed. Had an image in his mind of men falling around him, of gushing blood and of the feeling that his sword made cutting into flesh and bone. They had taken prisoners too. Hundreds, he supposed. Thousands, perhaps. The whole French column was gone, Bonaparte's great attack destroyed. And they had done it. The Greys. The Union Brigade. His reason told him that now they should stop, should reform the regiment, the brigade. But all around him the men were carrying on.

He saw Ponsonby, with his aide, De Lacy Evans. Shuldham rode across and suggested they might recall the brigade.

Ponsonby agreed but as the General spoke, Shuldham was aware that others had seen Ponsonby too and soon there was a crowd of some 30 redcoated dragoons around them, cheering and huzzaing. Ponsonby smiled and nodded, and began to lead them away from the enemy, back towards the lines, but at that moment Colonel Muter of the Inniskillings came roaring past, at full gallop, his sword pointed to the French, with 20 men of his regiment following. Ponsonby called to him, shouted. But the Colonel was too taken up with the battle to hear.

Almost instantly, and to a man, the dragoons of all three regiments who had collected about Ponsonby turned and were off behind Colonel Muter, to join the Irish. The General frowned, 'Well, I'll be damned. Damn the man. Come on. We'll stop them yet.'

Turning to follow Muter and the others, Ponsonby went off in pursuit, and Shuldham and Evans had no option but to follow.

After some distance, when they had passed between two ragged columns of French infantry and emerged close behind the Colonel and his dragoons, Shuldham was aware, that in the corner of his vision, to his left and rear, a body of cavalry was bearing down on them. He turned to face them and saw what he most dreaded.

He shouted to Ponsonby, 'Sir. Lancers. Lancers to your rear, Sir.' Shuldham turned to face the new threat and, trying to gain speed to meet them head-on, kicked his legs into his horse and found himself facing just one of them, as the others drove past him in pursuit of the General, the Greys and the Inniskillings.

The man came on towards him at a gallop and thrust his lance straight at Shuldham's horse's head. It missed; Shuldham made a cut at his adversary's arm as the two of them passed and only recovered to turn after a few yards. He wondered, had he hit him? Then he glimpsed the spatter of fresh blood on the man's white pouch belt and, turning fully, saw the Lancer clutching his wounded arm. But beyond the man he could see by the rise and fall of men and horses that the other Lancers had found their quarry. But of Ponsonby and his aide there was no sign.

✳

Corporal Dickson was riding hard. He had taken Kinchant's death badly and the hatred boiled inside him. Fired up to a frenzy, he had followed a wave of British dragoons up the enemy slope, towards the French Grand Battery. And now, urging each other on, they reached the crest, only to find themselves in a ploughed field of heavy clay. Within seconds too many of the horses were up to their knees. Their riders pushed and spurred, and slowly most of the beasts dragged themselves out, coated with mud.

Even though Rattler had by chance avoided the worst of it, Dickson could tell that she was fast becoming exhausted. But there was nothing for it now but to press on.

Galloping again towards the battery, they were joined by Colonel Hamilton who, now minus his headdress, was shouting at the top of his voice, 'Charge! Charge the guns!'

A few of the French cannon had loaded double cannister and let go at the first of the Greys and Inniskillings to reach them, hitting ranks of the dragoons with terrible effect. Ahead of him Dickson could see the impact. Horses and men thrown into the air and pushed over like skittles. He rode over the horribly mangled bodies of his comrades. Rattler's hooves became slick with blood and mud. And then he was in among the French guns. Those big twelve-pounders that had done such slaughter among the ranks. The Emperor's beautiful daughters, they called them. Now was time for their revenge.

Dickson and the others, the Colonel among them, set about the gunners with their sabres. He heard the

Frenchmen crying 'Diable!' as he struck, and the long-drawn out hiss that came through their teeth, as his sword went home.

*

The artillery drivers sat on their horses, weeping aloud as the Greys chopped and cut at them. Some were mere boys, thought Dickson. But still he went on.

Groups of gunners had formed and were trying to defend themselves against the dragoons, fighting off the cavalry with muskets and sabres and ramrods. Most, though, were either running for their lives or cowering beneath the carriages and limbers.

Dickson and the Greys gave no quarter. Were these not the men who had fired at them across the valley with such vigour throughout the day? The men who had accounted for so many dead among them and the infantry?

They fell upon the French gunners with a terrible, irrepressible fury, and the sabres sang and fell. Some of the drivers of the artillery train were hacked down as they ran, others froze to the spot with terror, and were sabred where they stood. The troopers stood high in their stirrups to give their already heavy blades more force on the down swing, causing terrible wounds. Some of those who surrendered were spared. But only a few. There was no reason or mercy here. No room for it.

The artillery horses met the same fate as their masters. Dickson heard someone shout 'Lame the horses. Attack the horses. Don't let them carry off the guns'. And so the troopers struck at the horses' flanks and thighs, sending them crashing down in a tangle of traces and bleeding flesh.

✳

Rattler seemed to have got new strength and had lost her temper in the noise of battle, biting and tearing at everything and anyone that came in her way. As they circled the guns, slashing down at the gunners, French infantry came pouring past them in droves, utterly disordered, on their way to the rear.

Suddenly, Armour shouted at him and pointed at Rattler. Looking down, Dickson realised, to his horror, that she had at last been wounded. A French bayonet had caught her on the chest and the gash had torn a muscle. Loathe as he was to do it, Dickson dismounted. He petted the mare as she sank heavily to her knees, and with whispered words of comfort in her ear, left her lying in the mud, alive, but in too much pain and far too tired to continue.

Looking around for a remount, Dickson saw a lone horse standing riderless, a French Colonel's mount. He caught hold of its reins, and springing up on its back, rode on. Armour shouted again and pointed to their left.

'Look, look there!' As Dickson looked, 200 yards away, he saw a group of French officers standing by a farmhouse, and among them a small figure in a grey coat. He stared, scarcely able to believe what he was seeing. Boney himself. He wanted to savour the moment, but knew that there was no time to stop, for turning back to the gunners, he noticed something in the valley below them. The tell-tale glint of sunlight on metal.

Two regiments of Cuirassiers had appeared on the right, in their sparkling steel breastplates and helmets, mounted on strong black horses, travelling at full gallop along the valley floor, while away to the left he could make out more horsemen, a regiment of Lancers.

The Cuirassiers, it seemed, were coming straight for them, tearing up the mud as they went. There was no doubting it. There was now a brigade's worth of fresh, French cavalry between them and their lines.

Dickson found Armour again. Where were their officers? Captain Vernor, Mister Mills?

Armour shook his head. 'God knows. Not seen 'em. All dead.'

Dickson looked at him, 'Come on then, Jimmy. Let's be at them.' Someone close by shouted, 'Come on, lads, that's the road home!' And with a score or more dragoons of all regiments with them, he and Armour sped down the hill.

He pushed the reluctant horse down the slope, riding as hard as he could away from the Cuirassiers, dashing his spurs into her sides, and setting course for the Lancers.

It was suicide and they all knew it. But what choice did they have? The Cuirassiers were fresh to the fight and big men on big horses. The Lancers on the other hand had already shot their bolt in their first counter-attack. But they still had some fight in them. Dickson was not the first to make contact with them and, as he watched, the lances rose and fell for a moment above the red-coated dragoons, and a man he knew, Corporal Sam Tar, a brickie from Biggleswade, out at the front of the Greys, fell in a flash of steel. Again, Dickson felt the rage rise in him.

He careered into the Lancers with a crash, the horses rearing and biting at each other. Two of the dragoons to his right were thrown and, rising to their feet, standing in the mud, tried to ward off the lances with their hands, but it was no use; the French went at them two and three to a man. Cornet Sturgis of the Royals came up to Dickson on the left, and Armour on his right.

Brought to a halt on their horses now, fetlock deep in the mud, they slashed at the Lancers, right and left, over the animals' necks.

A Lancer pushed towards Dickson, burying the point of his lance in his horse's breast. As she sank down, Dickson threw himself off and, sabre in hand, parried the thrusts of the Frenchman. Sturgis came up behind the man, and with a single deft cut, severed his right arm, sending him to the ground where he was trampled by the horses.

Then, grabbing the Lancer's horse by the bridle, the officer pulled it towards Dickson, who clambered up on to the sheepskin saddlecloth.

'Thought I was dead for certain, Sir. Much in your debt, Mister Sturgis.'

The Cornet nodded and smiled, and then took off again into the cavalry, in search of his own men. Much to Dickson's surprise, the Lancers were dispersing now, and making the most of the moment, he called to Armour, and together they sped off towards the Allied lines.

Taking care to skirt the edge of another ploughed field, riding on the grass by a hedgerow, Dickson stopped.

Just inside the field, and almost at his horse's hooves, lay the body of General Ponsonby, beside his little bay hack. His body bore the bloody marks of having been impaled by many lances. Never, thought Dickson, had such a courageous man been mounted on a horse less suited for battle. Ponsonby was lying on his back, his sightless eyes staring up at the sky. His long, fur-lined coat which he had worn over his scarlet tunic had blown aside. Dickson looked closer and saw something shining in his hand. His gold pocket watch. It was open, and within its lid was a miniature of a lady. Impossible, thought Dickson, but to look at him, you would say that the General had opened it to gaze on her as he died. Looking beyond him, Dickson saw other red-coated bodies and a few in green, and there, closest to Ponsonby, was another he recognised: Major Reignolds of his own regiment, the Brigade Major. His hand lay close to that of Ponsonby's which held the watch, and Dickson fancied that perhaps the General had been meaning to hand it to his aide when both had met their end.

Like Ponsonby, Reignolds had clearly been pierced by the Lancers, perhaps just a few moments before he and Armour had arrived at the scene. But there was worse to come, for just beyond Reignolds, while Armour carried on, Dickson saw a sight that filled his heart with sorrow.

Lieutenant Carruthers, three lance-wounds bleeding in his chest, side and lower leg, was lying on his back, his eyes open like the General's. But he was not dead. He turned his head towards Dickson and caught his eye with an expression that needed no words. Dickson was about to dismount to go to his aid, when there was a shout from his rear. Turning, he saw Sturgis and some of his men riding hard towards him, and behind them a mob of Lancers. The Cornet called to him, 'Go on, man, go on. Get away. Get back!'

Dickson needed no more urging. He dug his spurs into the new mount and, as she took off towards the Allied lines, managed a glance back at Carruthers. But the Lieutenant was no longer looking at Dickson. He too had seen the Lancers and was trying to drag himself through the mud, away from them. But three of them had found him; and not wanting to see the young officer stuck like a pig, Dickson looked away and rode for his life.

20

18 June, 2.30 pm
The Valley

Colonel James Hamilton realised at once what had happened, and in that very same instant knew that he was too late.

His horse had come to a halt, and it was as if the battle were unfolding all around him, leaving him as a spectator at some grand opera. He watched as his men fought with all the grit he had hoped for, slaughtering the French who were trying to shield their heads with their hands and being maimed for their trouble. But it was clear the Greys had gone too far. He had taken them up to the guns. It had been his decision and a good one. The battery that had caused so much suffering was as good as gone, with dead French gunners everywhere, their teams of horses ruined.

But Hamilton could see that his beloved Greys too might soon be lost. From where he sat, his head throbbing, his breathing heavy and hard, he was able to see beyond the melee, and the whole French right wing lay before him. Not just d'Erlon's infantry, who were still being cut to pieces, but beyond them, column after column, lining the road to Charleroi. Infantry in blue coats and some of them in long greatcoats, and to their right the cavalry. Thousands of them, Cuirassiers and Chasseurs, the great Guard Grenadiers in their bearskin hats and the red Lancers.

He wondered which of them Bonaparte would order to the counter-attack. The Cuirassiers in the valley had been merely a taster of the fury that would soon come. And as he watched, a brigade of Cuirassiers, their steel breastplates flashing in the sunshine, came up the slope towards the battery.

Seized with panic, Hamilton came back to his senses and looked for his men. A knot of the Greys, a corporal and three troopers, were together finishing off a ragged group of Frenchmen. Hamilton saw them pull away from the dying men and start to ride on. He screamed at them: 'Halt, halt, Greys. You must halt!' He was aware of a hand on his shoulder.

Lieutenant Gape. 'Sir, come away, Sir. You must come away. We must retire before it is too late.'

Hamilton looked at him, and then, without a word, pulled away from his hand and galloped into the French lines. If his men were going further then he surely would follow.

He struck home into a small improvised square of infantry and two cuts dealt with as many of the Frenchmen. The others turned and ran, and as they did so, Hamilton was aware of men to his left. Four Cuirassiers had appeared as if from nowhere and their leader, a huge moustachioed sergeant, was at him before he knew it.

Hamilton felt the blow that severed his left hand as if someone had hit him hard with a hammer. It was a dull pain and not at all what he had imagined it would be like to be cut to the bone with a sabre. Instinctively he wheeled round and took the man with a blow of his own sword, slicing deep into his arm so that it hung loose from the bone at the side of his armour. Gape was there to help him now, and two more of the Greys who had gone ahead. All of them hacking at the Cuirassiers.

Hamilton glanced down at the bloody stump and wondered that he felt no pain, but sensed that soon he must do. He seemed for a while to be living at a strangely slow pace. Every moment, every second, a minute of time. He knew that he must be in shock and pressed his thighs more tightly against the flanks of his mount, determined to remain in the saddle.

Seeing another gap in the press of men around him, he urged her forward and emerged in a clearing with two of the men, then looked around to see where the rest of his regiment might be. He saw his trumpeter, Buncle, and other men swinging round on grey horses, cutting furiously at the enemy around them. Then, pushing on further, he was aware of Sergeant Ewart on his left, making for the rear and carrying in his hand a tricolour topped with a French Eagle. An Eagle! Hamilton managed a cheer and shouted to the Sergeant but Ewart did not stop.

Galloping through a gap in the guns, still impervious to any pain from his severed hand, Hamilton saw what he had most dreaded. There on his left was a mass of green-coated, brass-helmeted Lancers, a brigade at least. They came on, swinging through what had been the Greys' left flank. Hamilton watched them at work, in pairs and threes, as they chased his men across the muddy ground and the bodies of the French. Saw the beautiful grey horses stumble and fail to rise as their riders were stuck like pigs.

One of his men rode up to him. It was Gape again, breathless and sweating and staring at the Colonel's mangled arm. Yet, although he could see his mouth opening and closing, Hamilton could not hear the words. Could hear nothing but a great roaring in his ears. His arm had begun to ache now. Worse by the second. He looked down at the ground, and in doing so noticed that his horse's left flank, a grey-white sheet of skin, was red with the gore from his wound. The floor of the valley below him was like a charnel house, with dead and dying Frenchmen everywhere, some piled on each other, where they had fallen. Gunners lay draped across their gun carriages. Horses too, their bodies torn with sabre-cuts. By God, but they had triumphed. The regiment, his regiment, had proven itself in battle and had taken an Eagle.

Another man was close to him now, shouting. Corporal Dickson.

Still deaf, Hamilton yelled at him, 'Dickson. Hurrah! An Eagle, Dickson, we have an Eagle!' Then seeing other men of his command and some from the Royals, he shouted to them, 'Greys, to me. North British, form on me!' He raised his sword in the air and once more, pushed in with his legs. The pain in his hand was coming on fast now. Searing. Dreadful. Conscious again of the helmeted, green-coated Lancers coming from his left, he sought out Dickson and found Buncle. 'Sound the alarm, man. Lancers to the left. Lancers left, mind your flank.' And then, seeing them coming for him: eight, no ten of them, galloping straight for him, Colonel James Hamilton pushed in his spurs and in seconds he was gone, his scarlet coat devoured by a sea of green.

*

Four hundred yards to his rear, Ewart found a gap in the melee and rode clear of the French. He must be nearly there now, surely? There was no clear line now, but there were redcoated infantry here and Highlanders with them, and up ahead, not two hundred yards away, the hedge line on the hill. Ewart rode on and then he saw them.

A group of half-a-dozen mounted men, all in blue uniforms, swords drawn and wearing bicorne hats, fore and aft, were riding straight for him. But he did not recognise their uniform. They were not Belgian, he thought, no orange sashes about them at all. And they were certainly not British. With mounting horror, he concluded that they must be French.

Ewart raised his sword, ready for the worst. Clearly the man to their front was a senior officer, covered as he was with gold bullion. He had a swarthy appearance, but at the same time he was smiling. And, Ewart saw now, while his companions were all armed with drawn sabres, this man had no weapon in his hand. Ewart understood. The man was a staff officer. The others his escort. He cursed his luck. How he had done it he had no idea, but clearly, he had ridden the wrong way, back into the French lines instead of towards his own.

A French general, dammit. Obviously, seeing him with the captured colour, the man had ridden across to retake it. But no one would have the Eagle. His Eagle. Ewart looked around, but saw that, once again, he was alone. Dickson and Armour were gone and, wherever the bulk of his regiment might be, the few men on grey horses he

could see, with others from the Royals and the Inniskillings, were streaming hell for leather back towards the
lines. Ewart reined his horse to the right and, desperate
to outride the blue-coated horsemen, pushed on. But he
had gone no further than a few yards when it became
clear they would catch him. There was nothing for it but
to stand.

*

The men were nearly on him now, and Ewart gripped his
sabre in his right hand as tight as the Eagle was held in his
left. At that moment a voice spoke, 'Hold there. General.
Hold fast.'

Ewart turned, to see behind him three of the Greys,
men he knew. They were advancing in line and behind the
man in the centre, propped against him in the saddle, was
Major Clarke. Clearly he was badly wounded. Nevertheless it was Clarke who called again. Told the General with
authority that to take the Eagle to the rear was Ewart's
honour and his alone. He had earned it.

As they drew closer to the General, he turned to the
Major. General Miguel d'Alava, Spanish Ambassador to
the Netherlands and one of Wellington's old Peninsular
comrades, was, for once, covered in confusion.

He smiled at Clarke, muttered words of apology. Of
course he must give it to the Duke. They would escort
him. His staff and himself. A guard of honour for the
brave 'serjente'. And the Major, he said, must attend to
his wounds.

Clarke said nothing, but frowned. Ewart could not
tell if it was mostly from pain or annoyance. His face

was quite white and he was breathing heavily. Ewart too remained mute. But in the awkward silence, one of the men, a corporal of the Greys, an Irishman by the name of Lynch, spoke up. 'Beggin' your pardon, Sir, but I think Sergeant Ewart would rather ride with us.'

Ewart fell in with the party and together, with Alava left red-faced on the field, they trotted carefully towards the rear, bearing both the colour and Major Clarke who, even in great pain, could not help but keep grinning at the Sergeant and his Eagle.

*

Ewart found Wellington, as Clarke had said he would, surrounded by a cloud of staff, close to the solitary elm tree that grew on the north side of the crossroads above the farm of la Haye Sainte. He would have known the Duke anywhere. There was the simple frock-coat, emblazoned with its Garter star, and the famous, familiar black bicorne, worn fore and aft and adorned with coloured cockades of all the Allies. And there, most obviously, was that nose that had given the beloved General the nickname that had haunted him through the Peninsula. 'Nosey' was deep in conversation with one of his aides but one of his staff, noticing Ewart approaching, pointed him out.

'Look, your Grace, look. A French Eagle.'

Wellington turned and stared at Ewart who, for a moment, caught his eye and was transfixed. But drawing closer, he managed a few deferential words.

The Duke doffed his hat. 'Sergeant. You have taken an Eagle. Well done, man. Well done.'

Wearing a huge smile, he turned to the staff. 'Look,

gentlemen. This man has an Eagle.' He looked back at Ewart, 'Who are you?'

'Sergeant Ewart, Sir. Scots Greys.'

'You're a credit to your nation, Ewart. Now take that bird and lodge it in the town hall at Brussels. And when I have won the battle I shall have it taken to the Prince Regent in London. And you will go with it and be presented.'

The Duke turned back to his aide and Ewart, a little unsure as to whether he was dismissed, looked nonplussed until motioned to leave by one of the staff officers. He nodded his head at the Duke in what he intended to be a bow, and, pulling on his reins, moved away from the knot of officers beneath the elm and down the slope on to the Brussels road. He took a last look down the road towards the French lines and saw before him a vision of hell. Men and horses caught up in a conflagration of smoke and flame, and everywhere the bodies of the dead and dying. He put up a silent prayer to his comrades and, turning his horse to the north, set out along the cobbled road to Brussels and salvation.

*

Back where Ewart had come from, in the mudbath that was now the base of the valley, John Dickson was again in trouble. A Frenchman's bayonet had wounded him in the lower leg. It was not deep but it was enough to be uncomfortable. Mounted unsteadily on the French officer's nag, he was trying to locate his regiment. She was a sluggish brute and he found that digging in his spurs was the only way to make her move.

He could see Armour, still mounted, a little way off, and making for him becoming caught in the mud. The French infantry were not bothering with him now, all of them streaming back towards their own lines. But just as he managed to kick his useless horse clear of the cloying mud, a lone Lancer came at him from the right and caught him with the tip of his lance on the same leg in which he had already been wounded. He managed to parry the shaft away before it was pushed home, but nevertheless the pain seared through him. The Lancer turned and letting his lance slip, drew his sabre to come at Dickson again, but he had not ridden more than a few yards when his face froze in a mask of pain. As Dickson watched a horseman rode from behind the Lancer, withdrawing his bloody sabre from the man's body as he came. He wore a bell-topped shako and a blue coat, and Dickson recognised him instantly as a British Light Dragoon.

Within seconds, more of his regiment, the 16th, were sweeping past Dickson and Armour, on their way after the French. who ran before them, Lancers and infantry together. Dickson cheered them on and, hearing other 'hurrahs', realised that the two of them were not alone as he had thought, but among dozens of dragoons from the brigade still in the valley. He rode, in some pain from his leg, to find Armour, and with scarcely a word passing between them, the two horsemen began to ride back together towards their own lines.

21

18 June, 3 pm
Mont St Jean

Having lost Colonel Hamilton in the melée, Lieutenant James Gape had come to his senses and ridden clear of the French, back across the valley. As he had come he had seen General Ponsonby surrounded by Lancers and had thought him taken prisoner. Circling now, close to the British line, he looked desperately for other members of the regiment before noticing Captain Fenton, with whom he had served in the 4th Light Dragoons in Spain.

He rode up to Fenton. The Captain looked at him, saw the familiar features and asked what news he might have.

'Colonel Hamilton's dead, Sir. Quite sure of it. Lost his hand. Cut off, before taking off into the French.'

Fenton said nothing but shook his head. Gape asked if he had seen his troop, but the Captain said that he had not. He seemed to Gape quite desolate at the news of the Colonel.

Alone again, Gape searched for Macmillan, and after some minutes caught sight of De Lacy Evans.

He hailed him and Evans rode across, 'Lieutenant?'

'Gape, Sir, of the Greys. I saw the General, Sir. General Ponsonby. He has been made prisoner, Sir.'

Evans queried the comment. 'You're sure? I saw General Ponsonby myself in a field quite close to here.' He pointed towards it, 'There. You're sure he's a prisoner?'

Gape was adamant.

Evans was suddenly animated, 'We must rescue him, Gape. I'll find some men. Ride to General Somerset and tell him what has happened. Request a troop of the Household Cavalry. We must do what we can to rescue General Ponsonby.'

Gape rode across the main road towards the Allied right and there, close to the elm tree that marked the Duke's command post, he found Somerset and two of his staff surveying the battlefield, their horses panting with exhaustion and flecked with mud and sweat.

Major Evans, he said, had sent him to request assistance with the view of recovering General Ponsonby, and such other of their officers and men who were in the hands of the French.

Somerset shook his head.

'That is most unfortunate. Most unlucky. Poor Sir William. I did warn him to take a better horse. Still, made prisoner. That's not so bad. They will exchange him ere long. We must surely have enough senior officers of theirs among all this.'

He indicated a large mass of French infantry who were being herded to the rear of the Allied lines by a troop of Hussars.

Somerset looked at Gape. 'But you see I really can do nothing for you. My brigade is gone, Sir.'

Looking around him now, Gape could see that this was evident. Apart from a group of a score or so from the Blues and a similar group of the Life Guards, along with a number of wounded, Somerset's Household Brigade had effectively ceased to exist. For the time being at least. It was clear that Somerset was in shock, unable to believe that the finest cavalry in the world had been scattered to the winds.

Gape took his leave politely, and seeing a Hanoverian hussar regiment drawn up to the rear, approached their Colonel, asking him in French if they would come with him to save their General. But the man laughed and replied that, as he had no orders to do such a thing, he would not do it.

Gape rode off, and spying General Vandeleur thought it worth chancing his luck in a similar request. But the General shook his head and said that he had no orders yet to charge.

So Gape had no choice but to ride back to the crossroads. But when he got there, of De Lacy Evans there was no sign, and at length, a little way off to the north, standing on their horses in the lee of the reverse slope, he found what was left, he presumed, of the Greys.

Sergeant Bishop, the recently appointed Quartermaster, was with them. Gape enquired as to their strength.

Bishop told him that Captain Cheney was in command, with Captain Payne as his second. Major Clarke had been badly wounded and was back at the Farm with Lieutenant Hamilton and Lieutenant Wemyss. It was said that Clarke might lose his arm. And there were sixty troopers left. Trotter was dead, Kinchant and Shuldham were missing, and Barnard and Major Poole as well.

Gape was shocked. Sixty troopers. And his friends all dead and wounded, and that after one action.

Bishop spoke again. Lieutenant Mills was with them, though, and had said that he had seen Cornet Westby taken by the Lancers, as was Mister Graham.

Gape enquired about Wyndham and Vernor. Bishop said nothing, and Gape took it to be the worst sort of news.

Finally he asked Bishop how the Brigade had fared.

'They say there's only a hundred and thirty of us left all told, Sir.'

'Of all three regiments of the Brigade?'

'Yes, Sir.'

A hundred and thirty men of the three regiments that had counter-attacked the French. It was impossible, thought Gape. Why, that would mean that some ninety percent of their strength were dead, wounded or missing. Over a thousand men.

Gape looked at the faces of the men around Bishop and saw nothing but exhaustion. They were pale to a man, but weathered with mud, traces of blood and dried sweat.

The Adjutant, Lieutenant Henry Macmillan, came up to him, and asked if he had seen his cloak, which he was holding out before him. Gape looked at it and saw that it had been holed in several places by musket balls. Macmillan laughed and blessed his good luck. His horse, Nelly, he said, had been wounded, shot in the shoulder. He had not been able to find her.

*

The next hour passed as quickly as the previous two had been slow. Gape was aware of being ordered to retire behind a wood.

They would be safe here, he thought, and confident that with their horrendous casualties they would not be asked to go again that day, he watched as the enemy's shot and shells passed overhead. Clearly, too, the first casualty reports had been somewhat exaggerated. There must have been, he thought, about a hundred and fifty of the Greys here alone now, from the four hundred and forty who had attacked the French. It was bad, but not as bad as it had at first seemed. Losses among the officers, though, appeared to have been particularly heavy. With Colonel Hamilton gone and Major Clarke badly wounded, the newly created Colonel Cheney was now in command.

22

Situation Report
18 June, 4 pm

As the Greys were regrouping, there now occurred the most celebrated event of the day and certainly the most confused. It lasted for around two hours and has gone down in the annals as one of the great blunders of military history.

From around 3 pm, Wellington, seeing the terrible damage that the French guns were doing, pulled his army back from the slope on to the fields in the reverse.

Down in the valley, Marshal Ney, leading an attack at 3.30 pm against La Haye Sainte saw the movement, and may have thought to exploit it. He sent an aide to summon a brigade of Cuirassiers to penetrate what he saw must be a gap in the British line.

And the Cuirassiers came, in their thousands. The first phase of what was to become a major attack included Milhaud's entire Cuirassier corps with the elite Imperial Guard Light Cavalry of Lancers and Chasseurs. It began at 4 pm with almost 5,000 horsemen moving up the slope in the gap between, on their right the central farm of La Haye Sainte, and to their left the orchard walls of Hougoumont.

Cresting the ridge, however, they found, not the expected gap and a retreating army, but Wellington's infantry, drawn up in a chequerboard pattern of defensive squares, almost impossible to penetrate. Once there, however, there was no going back and the cavalry began to attack. It was carnage.

The chessboard formation allowed the cavalry to flow through, exposing them to a murderous cross-fire. The gunners fired their pieces as the cavalry closed, then ran back into the cover of the squares. Ney, who led the attack, had three horses shot from under him. And gradually more and more French cavalry were sucked into the attack.

✳

An hour later, General Kellerman's Corps of Cuirassiers, with dragoons and carabiniers among them, was drawn in with the Guard Heavy Cavalry: the Grenadiers à Cheval, Napoleon's 'Gods' on their huge black horses, and the Empress Dragoons. Another 4,500 men went thundering up the hill against the British and Allied squares.

There is a theory that the debacle was not Ney's fault, but the action of a red Lancer officer that brought in all the cavalry, and according to this it would seem that it was less a programmed attack and more a mass frenzy to get at the British which committed all 10,000 cavalry, condemning most of them to death.

✳

Neither was it any picnic inside the Allied squares. Before each charge the French artillery opened up on the squares, even though they could not be seen. The effect on the closely-packed formations was devastating. And then the cavalry would appear.

Gronow recalled: 'You perceived at a distance what appeared to be an overwhelming long moving line which, ever advancing, glittered like a stormy wave of the sea when it catches the sunlight . . . The word of command, Prepare to receive cavalry, had been given. Every man in the front rank knelt, and a wall bristling with steel, held together by steady hands, presented itself to the infuriated Cuirassiers.'

He also described a square: 'Inside we were nearly suffocated by the smoke and smell from burnt cartridges. It was impossible to move a yard without treading on a wounded comrade or upon the bodies of the dead, and the loud groans of the wounded and dying were most appalling. At four o'clock our square was a perfect hospital, being full of dead, dying and mutilated soldiers.'

In fact it was worse than this. Soldiers were too tired to keep their muskets level. Many would have had dislocated shoulders from firing all day. The smell was awful, of excrement, vomit, blood and acrid smoke that choked the lungs. Faces were black from powder.

Behind the squares, though, the Allied light cavalry were ready to counterattack as required, and eventually the French attacks stopped. Only at 5.30 pm was French infantry support sent in, in the form of Bachelu's and Foy's divisions. But it was too late. The French had squandered their heavy cavalry.

All along the Allied line the air was now a mass of shot and bullets. Men compared it to the humming of a swarm of bees.

23

18 June, 5 pm
The Rear of the Crossroads, Mont St Jean

They had been standing in the wood for around an hour, when an aide galloped up with fresh orders, and soon young Ensign Gape found himself in command of a squadron; one of only three into which the reduced-strength regiment had been re-formed. He realised also that, as it was being reformed, his idea that they would not be needed again was to be proved wrong. So it was no surprise when shortly afterwards another aide came up with the order that the second brigade should be brought up again.

They crossed the Brussels road some distance behind the crossroads and close to the farm of Mont St Jean, which was now filled with the wounded. From there they advanced to the reverse of a slope on what was the right of the Allied line and there they halted once again.

John Bishop was with them. Looking around at his once splendid regiment, he saw a unit transformed. So many of the great grey horses had been killed and lost that he observed that the regiment no longer deserved the title 'Greys', for such were the remounts they had obtained that they were now naught but a motley assemblage of bays and duns.

At around 5 pm Bishop watched the Earl of Uxbridge ride in front of the Brigade. Uxbridge, resplendent in his gold trimmed shako and the blue and gold uniform of a cavalry general, addressed them: 'Come on my brave boys, let us cut them up to a man.'

With Cheney at their head, and flanked by the remnants of the other regiments of the Brigade, they followed Uxbridge who led them in an attempt at a charge.

Their target was a square of infantry over on their left, close to the farm of La Haye Sainte, and Bishop noticed the Life Guards joining them on their right flank. It was just as well, for with the French infantry had come French Cuirassiers, who now occupied the ground between the two regiments of British cavalry, beyond the flanks of which lay squares of Hanoverian infantry. Bishop thought it like a game of chess and wondered if the battle might be lost.

As they spurred on towards the French, the square before them opened up with a volley which brought down men all round Bishop. Nevertheless, they smashed into the French cavalry and threw them back, but in the swirling melee, Bishop saw the Life Guards pulled apart by the Cuirassiers.

The trumpeter sounded the recall and the Greys pulled back to the slope. Again Bishop was conscious of how few of them remained. Standing again on the reverse slope behind the crossroads, Bishop could feel his horse shaking with the exertion and was conscious too of the sweat running down his back and face beneath the tall bearskin cap.

For another full hour they stood there. Surely, he thought, that will be our portion for the day. But even as the thought crossed his mind, he realised that something in him said that if asked to go again he would have done so readily. Suddenly, to their front, the hillside was broken by cheering and the cries of officers of infantry giving the command to form line from square.

This, Bishop knew, could only mean one thing. The threat of cavalry had passed. And the cheering was stronger now.

Bishop saw a rider approach Cheney, and being close by, he heard the message. The Prussians were on the field. Blücher was here. The commanding officer's voice rang out to their front, 'The regiment will advance.'

And, their swords shouldered and at a trot, the Greys advanced up the slope, the landscape to the south of the field gradually opening up as they crested the hill. As they did so a terrifying sight met Bishop's eyes. Never before had he beheld such carnage. As far as the eye could see lay men and animals, while through them lines of redcoated British and Hanoverians, the blue coats of Belgium and the green of Nassau and jet-black Brunswickers were advancing towards the French. But still their cannon fired, and even as he watched a man of the Royals was taken away from his saddle by a roundshot. A shell burst nearby and Bishop cowered instinctively. He was giving thanks for deliverance when his horse collapsed and threw him, so that he was trapped beneath her. Trying to stand, he saw that a shell splinter had pierced her chest. Two dragoons dragged him out from beneath her, and cursing himself for having lost a second grey, he looked for another mount. He found one without much trouble, but she was a bay.

Again Uxbridge came up to them, and through his staff, the two brigades, the Life Guards and what was left of the Union Brigade, were formed into one squadron.

Again Uxbridge led them on, and again they charged the Cuirassiers to their front. After the shock of impact they stood no more than forty yards from the French, who did the same, and fired at each other with their carbines. But as this went on the French brought up their horse guns and unlimbered at close range. Bishop prepared for the worst, but was not ready for the grape shot which hit the squadron, which appeared to have been mixed in with broken glass and nails and caused some dreadful wounds.

The Greys and the others pulled back again, passing by the squares of British and Hanoverian infantry, who seemed, he thought, to flinch under the enemy cannon-fire, but were prevented from running by the shouts of their officers.

*

Lieutenant Archibald Hamilton had had as bloody a battle as anyone, and he was surprised to be still in the saddle. Covered in black powder, running with sweat and mud, he wheeled round from the second charge and cantered back towards the British lines.

Uxbridge had arrived back there before him and was sitting with a knot of his staff around him watching the battle, when Hamilton saw a cannonball fly in and strike the General on the leg.

The force of the shot lifted him off his horse, and so displaced he toppled from the saddle. Hamilton halted.

He was aware that all around him the battle seemed to be going against the Allies.

Again the French sent out cavalry skirmishers, who rode close up to the dragoons and fired their pistols in their faces; they returned fire with their carbines over their horses' heads at the French. In the midst of the fire-fight, one of the Greys, Hamilton wasn't sure who, was shot dead. At the same time the command was given for the regiment to retire twenty yards, out of range of the French pistols. As they did so, the dead man rode with them sitting on his horse, quite upright, yet completely dead. Fearing that such a horrendous sight might have a bad effect upon the men, Hamilton called to two of them to take him down and carry him to the rear.

24

Situation Report
18 June, 7 pm

Wellington's line was holding, but only just. Throughout the day the French had continued to attack Hougoumont, but the Guards had held out and were still doing so, tying up an entire French corps. In the centre too, at La Haye Sainte, the French had attacked all day and it had only been half an hour earlier at 6.30 pm that the farm had finally fallen.

The 13th French Light Infantry had poured in after an assault from the west broke through a rear gate into the barn and stables at the same time as French sappers had forced the main gate. The garrison, formed by the loyal Hanoverians of the King's German Legion, retreated with terrible losses. Of the 800 men sent in, only half came out alive. The French, though, had probably suffered double that loss, and as at Hougoumont, Major Baring's 800 Germans had tied up over 3,000 French.

*

From Wellington's position it seemed as if the French might now at last have the initiative. They were bringing up horse artillery to the farmhouse now, and the Duke knew that soon they would fire canister into the remaining British and Allied troops. He looked across to the left and wondered how long Blücher might take to reach him. For that now was his only hope.

Napoleon knew that too. From 1 pm he had been able to see Prussians approaching in the woods to his right. He had sent cavalry to block them, a regiment of hussars, and then detached Lobau's corps to the fields on the south east of Papelotte Farm, Wellington's easternmost strongpoint.

He was right to be worried. But the Prussians were heading for the village of Plancenoit deep in Napoleon's right flank, and Wellington was still exposed. It was only the desperate action of a British staff officer, who begged General Ziethen to change his line of march towards Wellington, that prevented disaster as the French prepared to roll up the Duke's flank.

From 4.30 pm General von Bulow's IV Corps of Prussians came on to the field, and from 6 pm onwards a battle raged around the village of Plancenoit.

Now, perceiving a last chance as Wellington's thin line bowed under pressure from the artillery bombardment, Napoleon at last led the Imperial Guard forward, and only just south of La Haye Sainte was persuaded to hand over command to Ney.

The Guard attacked in squares supported by cavalry and horse artillery. Some of the old grumblers, Napoleon's bearskin-wearing Grenadiers and Chasseurs, reached the ridge and attempted to deploy into line to meet the redcoats.

Wellington's line battalions had been decimated but they still gave fire as did the 1st Guards under Maitland.

Ney lost a fifth horse shot from under him, and marched up on foot with the Grenadiers.

But in a matter of minutes it was over. Fire from the ranks of the combined 33rd/69th and 30th/73rd regiments broke the 4th and 1st Imperial Guard Grenadiers who were then charged by fresh units of Dutch Belgians. Fire from the 1st Guards turned the 3rd Chasseurs and the 4th Chasseurs were blown to pieces on being taken in the flank by the British 52nd Light Infantry, the strongest battalion on the field.

As the Guard broke, Wellington waved his hat in the air three times and signalled a general advance.

*

Meanwhile, at Plancenoit, Lobau was being pushed back. At 6.45 pm Napoleon sent in the Young Guard who retook it only to lose it. At 7.15 pm two battalions of the Old Guard took the village back. But it was all in vain, and finally at 8 pm, as the Prussians arrived in overwhelming numbers, Plancenoit fell for the last time.

25

18 June, 9 pm
The Ridge of Mont St Jean

As dusk descended on the battlefield, Lieutenant Archibald Hamilton looked to the left of his regiment and was able plainly to perceive the flashes of the Prussian guns in the rear of the French army. He searched for his pocket watch but couldn't find it in his coat, which was so cut around that he thought it must have lost its pockets. He reckoned that from the sky and the light, it must have been close to eight o'clock when the French began to retire. They had been on the field under fire for some nine hours.

Hamilton looked around for the Scots Greys and saw very few men. Taking the time to count the other dragoons of the Brigade, he was horrified to discover that he could see no more than 33 officers and men, of the morning's total of 1,300.

It was now after nine o'clock at night, and everywhere the Allied line was advancing. For the Greys, though, there was to be no moment of glory. They were dispersed across the whole battlefield and beyond, lost as any sort of coherent unit.

Hamilton heard firing, but had no idea as to from where it came. It was too dark to see anything clearly. He could hear 'huzzas' as charges were made by the British Light Cavalry upon the retreating enemy and in the darkness had no alternative but to continue to advance along the right of the road by which the French retired. Suddenly he heard a voice calling out, 'Are you English?'

Hamilton answered that they were. 'Then,' said the voice, 'get over here, if you will. Here is a captain of the Dragoons badly wounded.'

Hamilton moved towards the voice, and saw an officer of the Inniskillings lying with a gaping wound in his side. He turned and rode back, and finding one of the Irish Dragoons, sent him to carry the officer back to Brussels.

A short while later Hamilton was ordered back to the village of Waterloo to collect the stragglers, and to bring them up the next day. With him went Lieutenant James Graham of Fenton's Troop, the youngest officer in the regiment at just sixteen. On the way, trotting as briskly as they could, the two men overtook a captain of the Royal Horse Artillery whom he knew, and who was on his way to Brussels. Hamilton rode with him to Waterloo, and asked him if he would be kind enough to inform a cousin of his in the same corps that he was safe.

Arriving in the village, Hamilton and Graham entered a large house, which they took correctly for an inn, and were confronted by a butcher's shop of dead and dying men. Oblivious to the carnage around them, but only too aware of the incessant groaning, they sat down to rest and ordered bread and wine from the innkeeper.

As soon as the wine arrived they began to talk over the events of the day. Who had fallen and who had survived. Graham attempted a head count of those whom he knew for certain were left of them: three officers, two sergeants and sixteen privates.

Hamilton noted that besides them there were wounded at the farm, and the men they believed had been taken prisoner, and others who were watching the French prisoners, on the road to Brussels. That was at least four score.

Graham agreed, but it still seemed to him that the regiment was gone. They had killed the regiment. Colonel James, Major Reignolds, Carruthers, Trotter too. Westby, Kinchant, Shuldham. All of them. The whole regiment had gone.

Hamilton nodded. They had been killed, of that there was no doubt. But then he looked hard at Graham, and reminded him that no matter how many of its men you might kill, and no matter how many of its officers, you couldn't kill a regiment.

Waterloo would be the making of them.

26

Postscript

The 19th of June dawned grey over the field of Waterloo. The sun had risen in the watery sky at 3.45 am, and already the looters were out picking at the dead and wounded for whatever riches they could find.

Hamilton and Graham returned to the field, bringing with them the stragglers from Waterloo. As they arrived at the hamlet of Mont St Jean, they found local peasants plundering a number of baggage wagons, which stood in the yard of one of the houses. As they watched, Hamilton was pleased to see more men from the regiment walking towards them from the direction of the battlefield. Among them was his servant, who had come up earlier from the rear to look for his body, having been informed by two different officers of the Brigade whom he had met on their way to Brussels, that Hamilton had been killed.

Hamilton and Graham spent the day burying the men of their regiment. Among them were eight officers. Trotter was the first. He had been shot through the heart. Graham had personally supervised the burial of Shuldham, whose body had been discovered on the field.

Hamilton made a note to write to Trotter's brother-in-law, offering to pay his bills and remit home the money that remained from his things being sold. He had lost many of his own possessions in the battle, but the day had one good outcome, in his purchase, for the bargain price of £55, of Colonel Hamilton's second horse, a lovely five year old, 'fit to carry fifteen stone'.

*

As Hamilton delighted in his purchase, John Dickson pondered the fate of her former owner. Colonel Hamilton's body had been found with both his arms cut off. His pockets had been rifled. He thought it an ignoble end for such a brave gentleman.

Gradually the true details of their losses began to filter through, along with what they had achieved. Major Clarke had two horses shot under him, and had been wounded himself. Lieutenant Charles Wyndham had been shot twice, once through the foot, but would recover. Captain James Poole had had a horse killed and been wounded five times, and had himself for some time been a prisoner of the French. Captain Robert Vernor's horse was shot through the head and he himself through the shoulder, both apparently by the same ball. He had found Colonel Hamilton's sword on the field and carried it back. Lieutenant James Wemyss had been badly wounded and his horse shot. Captain (now brevet Colonel) Cheney had had five horses shot under him (only one being his own, the rest taken from troopers). Only two officers, Captain Payne and Colonel Cheney, had escaped without being touched. They had lost 16 officers out of 24 on the field. Corporal Dickson had been wounded twice, while aiding Sergeant Ewart in his capture of the Eagle.

They found Troop Sergeant Major Weir of Fenton's troop lying dead on the field, and with typical coolness

Fenton told Graham to have his name written in his blood on his forehead so that they would know he was dead and not missing. He had, after all, been in charge of all the troop's money.

As the stories circulated, it emerged that the Brigade had smashed three columns of 15,000 men, captured two Imperial Eagles, and had stormed and rendered useless for a time more than 40 of the enemy's cannon. Besides that, they had taken nearly 3,000 prisoners. But more than all this, their charge and their sacrifice had saved the infantry of Picton's division from being wiped out and in doing so had saved the left wing of Wellington's army from being rolled up by the French. They had not won the battle but they had stopped the French, and bought Wellington time when he most needed it. Their part in his victory had been second to none.

Bibliography

Unpublished

Allison, James, Allison Album, RSDG Museum, Vol. C, Scots Greys at Waterloo

Smith, Dr J., Sergeant Ewart and the Scots Greys at Waterloo, RSDG Museum

Primary sources

Scots Greys Museum, with reference number:

G167   Bishop, John, Diary, June 1815
G350   Clarke, Major Isaac, Letter
G171   Ewart, Charles, Anecdotes
G348   Ewart, Charles, Letter, *c*.1840
G179   Hamilton, Archibald, At Waterloo with the Royal Scots Greys, published in *The Napoleonic Archive*
G152   The life of Colonel Inglis Hamilton
G179   Smith, Jeffrey, Sergeant Ewart and the Scots Greys at Waterloo
G152   Hozier, Notes on Cornet JC Kinchant
G179   Russell, James, Maj., Letter to his wife, transcript
G163   Wyndham, Lt. Col. C., Reminiscences of the battle of Waterloo, a letter

Boulter, Samuel, An Eye witness account of the Battle of Waterloo, published in *The Scots Grey* (regimental magazine), 1955

Dickson, John, Reminiscences of Waterloo, published in *The Scots Grey*, 1948 and 1961

Gape, James, Letter to his mother, 1815, published in *The Scots Grey*, 1950

Other regiments

Clay, Matthew, Adventures at Hougoumont, *Household Brigade Magazine* (1958)

Mercer, Cavalié, Journal of the Waterloo Campaign (1870)

Kincaid, J., Adventures in the Rifle Brigade (1830)

Gronow, R. H.,   The Reminiscences and Recollections of Captain Gronow (1889)

Leeke, William, The History of Lord Seaton's Regiment at the Battle of Waterloo (1866)

Martin, Jacques, Lettre d'un officier genevois du 45e in La Sabretache (1895)

Secondary sources

Adkin, Mark, *The Waterloo Companion* (2001)

Almack, Edward, *History of the 2nd Dragoons* (1908)

Coppens, Bernard, *Le Chemin d'Ohain, Waterloo 1815* (1999)

Dalton, Charles, *The Waterloo Roll Call* (1978)

Fosten, Bryan, *Wellington's Heavy Cavalry* (1982)

Glover, Gareth, *Letters from the Battle of Waterloo* (2004)

Grant, Charles, *Royal Scots Greys* (1972)

Hamilton-Williams, David, *Waterloo, New Perspectives* (1999)

Haythornwaite, P. J., *Waterloo Men* (1999)

Mackenzie, Peter, *Old Reminiscences of Glasgow* (1865)

Mellor, Stuart, *Greys' Ghosts* (2012)

Miller, David, *The Duchess of Richmond's Ball* (2004)

Robinson, Mike, *The Battle of Quatre Bras 1815* (2009)

Siborne, H. T., *Waterloo Letters* (1891)

Weller, Jac, *Wellington at Waterloo* (1967)